THE MYSTERY GUEST

60

FARRAR
STRAUS
GIROUX

© Sophie Calle

THE
MYSTERY GUEST

•

GRÉGOIRE BOUILLIER

Translated from the French by Lorin Stein

Farrar, Straus and Giroux / New York

Farrar, Straus and Giroux
19 Union Square West, New York 10003

Copyright © 2004 by Éditions Allia, Paris
Translation copyright © 2006 by Lorin Stein
All rights reserved
Distributed in Canada by Douglas & McIntyre Ltd.
Printed in the United States of America
Originally published in 2004 by Éditions Allia, France,
as *L'Invité mystère*
Published in the United States by Farrar, Straus and Giroux
First American edition, 2006

"De la Littérature considérée comme une tauromachie,"
by Michel Leiris, is quoted from Richard Howard's translation of
Manhood (New York: North Point Press, 1984).

Library of Congress Cataloging-in-Publication Data
Bouillier, Grégoire.
  [Invité mystère. English]
  The mystery guest / Grégoire Bouillier ; translated
by Lorin Stein.— 1st American ed.
    p.   cm.
  "Originally published in 2004 as L'invité mystère by Éditions
  Allia, Paris."
  ISBN-13: 978-0-374-18570-1 (hardcover : alk. paper)
  ISBN-10: 0-374-18570-0 (hardcover : alk. paper)
  I. Stein, Lorin.   II. Title.

PQ2702.O82I58 2006
843'.92—dc22

                                                    2006011403

Designed by Jonathan D. Lippincott

www.fsgbooks.com

1   3   5   7   9   10   8   6   4   2

This book was made possible in part by an investment from the
Literary Ventures Fund.

*Cet ouvrage, publié dans le cadre d'un programme d'aide à la publi-
cation, bénéficie du soutien du Ministère des Affaires étrangères et
du Service Culturel de l'Ambassade de France aux Etats-Unis.*

This work, published as part of a program of aid for publication,
received support from the French Ministry of Foreign Affairs and
the Cultural Services of the French Embassy in the United States.

The translator wishes to thank Violaine Huisman for her invalu-
able tutelage, encouragement, and editorial advice. Without her
this translation would not have been completed, or attempted.

To Sophie Calle

For reasons the reader will understand, I have neglected to translate the expression *"C'est le bouquet."*

It means, more or less, "That takes the cake."

I

It was the day Michel Leiris died. This would have been late September 1990, or maybe the very beginning of October, the date escapes me (whatever it was I can always look it up later on); in any case it was a Sunday, because I was home in the middle of the afternoon, and it was cold out, and I'd gone to sleep in all my clothes, wrapped up in a blanket, the way I generally did when I was home by myself. Cold and oblivion were all I was looking for at the time, but this didn't worry me. Sooner or later, I knew, I'd rejoin the world of the living. Just not yet. I felt I had seen enough. Beings, things, landscapes . . . I had enough to last me for the next two hundred years and saw no reason to go hunting for new material. I didn't want any more trouble.

•

I woke to the ringing of the phone. Darkness had fallen in the room. When I picked up I knew it was her. Even before I was conscious of knowing, I knew. It was her voice, her breath, it was practically her face, and along with her face came a thousand moments of happiness rising from the past, gilded with sunlight, caressing my own face and licking at my fingers while a thousand more like them swung at the other end of a wire.

•

I sat up in bed, heart pounding in my chest. I actually heard this going on, this unnatural pounding, as if my heart were electrified. I heard it thudding in every corner of the room—and this was no illusion, I wasn't dreaming, there wasn't any question of its being anyone but her. The senses don't lie, unlikely as it was to be hearing her voice now, after all the years I'd never heard from her, ever, not once. *How appropriate* flashed through my mind. *And on the exact same day Michel Leiris died* was my next thought, and the coincidence struck me as so outlandish it was all I could do to keep from laughing. I felt as if I'd tapped in to the inner hilarity of things, or else brushed up against a truth so overwhelming only a fit of hysterics could keep it at bay; but maybe it wasn't a coincidence at all. Maybe she wouldn't have called, it occurred to me, if Michel Leiris hadn't died. Of course that's what had happened: she'd heard about Michel Leiris and somehow the fact of his disappearance had made *her* reappear. However obscurely the one fact figured in the other, I sensed a connection. The significance of a dream, we're told, has less to do with its overt drama than with the details; a long time ago it struck me that the same was true of real life, of what passes among us for real life.

•

But this was no time for a philosophical discussion, and besides, I wasn't in any shape to bandy wits. I could hear how soft and gummy my voice was, how drowsy-sounding, and without even giving it any thought I realized that she must under no circumstance be allowed to know she'd woken me up. That was crucial, even if it meant sounding cold and detached—and why on earth did she have to call, not just on the very same day Michel Leiris had died but when I was fast asleep and at my most vulnerable, my least up to answering the phone, when in a word I was completely incapable of appreciating this miracle for what it was? In real life, it goes without saying, the ideal situation eludes us, and no doubt that's a good thing for humanity in general, but just then I'd have done anything to keep her from guessing that she'd caught me sound asleep in the middle of the afternoon. It was out of the question. Either it would seem like a sign of weakness or else it would make me look churlish, to be caught napping the one time something exceptional actually happened, or then again she might draw certain conclusions—I didn't know what conclusions, exactly, but still, I'd just as soon she not draw them. And no, I wanted to say, it wasn't as if my life had devolved into one long slumber. It wasn't as if I'd been languishing, stricken and alone, since she'd left me. On the contrary. I happened to be leading a life of leisure. I was in the pink. I was stopping to smell the roses, as the song so eloquently puts it, and couldn't imagine why she might think otherwise.

•

Here was the strangest part: I completely forgot that I'd sworn never to speak to her again, and that she'd left me years before without a word of explanation, without so much as saying goodbye, the way they abandon dogs when summer comes (as I put it to myself at the time), the way they abandon a dog chained to a tree for good measure. And I'd circled my tree in both directions and climbed up into it and spent a long time—spent millions of hours, years—in the void, cursing her name in the darkness. Yes, cursing her, because her disappearance had taught me that I was a less exemplary person than I'd thought; but now the whole thing might as well never have happened and all that mattered was the fact of her calling, and that the day for action had come.

•

How I had yearned for this moment! I'd been looking forward to it so long I already knew how it would go. I even knew what she was about to say because I'd rehearsed it all in my head, I could see myself softly explain that the past was the past, that the statute of limitations had expired, that it didn't matter that she'd left me (or that she'd left me the *way* she'd left me), it was ancient history. Really and truly. I'd dug down to the root of my unhappiness and it had nothing to do with her, I didn't blame her in the least, and in this cruel world we're all innocents, we all do the best we can, and worse things are happening all around us even as we speak. Just this morning Michel Leiris had died, and yesterday the last of the Mohawks had laid down his arms, and tomorrow a war and/or scandal would break out and be replaced by something else, and in the end the world would turn the page before I did, and it didn't exactly speak well of me that I'd taken years to get over her, and it's not as if I was talking about the Movie of the Week, where love triumphs, justice gets handed down, liberty's reestablished in the hearts of men, humanity regains a name and a face and the whole thing happens between 8:45 and 10:30, 10:35 at the latest—once I watched them save the earth from a giant meteor and even *that* didn't take two hours—and I'm not the sort of person who mixes up real life and fiction, no more than anybody else does, but the conviction had snuck up on me that I, too, would smile again in my own ninety minutes, give or take. Yes, I'd be smiling again in a more or less similar lapse of time; her leaving had been a blip. There was something crazy about how far it had set me back. In retrospect, the insane way she'd disappeared actually seemed for the best. It showed panache, at any rate, when most relationships just fizzle out as if they'd never happened. And I agreed with her, that was the thing, I agreed that she'd been fighting for her life. We couldn't go on the way we'd been, and she'd been driven to get out by nothing less than the survival instinct, and she was sorry, so she told me she was sorry and asked me in a whisper to forgive her, and it made me want to cry, to let the tears run down my cheeks, hearing her ask over and over how she could have just *left*, after four years together, after all we'd lived through, all we'd shared; but she'd had no choice. She was in so much pain. And she was so young and felt so guilty, without knowing why, she felt guilty all the time—I'd never know how guilty she felt—and maybe it was society's fault, maybe it was the fault of her family, she didn't know, but in the end she did the only thing she could and went off with the first man who wanted her. And he was a nice man, and he loved her, and she loved him, too, despite his age and the fact that he was short, and now they had a little girl, and she was happy I saw it the way I did because (and she knew I'd laugh) she kept worrying that I might have turned into a bum.

Sometimes on the bus she'd look out for me on city benches. She had this feeling that things had gone badly for me and it scared her. For years she'd been afraid of bumping into me. I had no idea how long it had taken just getting up the nerve to call, and tracking me down wasn't easy either, and in the end she just wanted me to know how sorry she really was and to forgive her. I had to understand, it meant the world to her. And I understood. I was all understanding. And I forgave, for in my dreams I was great and magnanimous. And besides, what else could I say or do?

•

But this was her actual voice, not just some figment that I'd invented to fill the void and salve my wounds, as they say; finally I'd hear her version, finally she'd come out and ask my forgiveness and acknowledge the thing she'd done. I pictured her hand gently closing my eyelids so I could open them freely on other sights and love again with no second thoughts. Yes, she owed me an explanation—she owed me *something* at any rate, some kind of redemption, something to seal the tomb and lay the remains of our affair to rest and mow down the weeds and nettles that had grown up inside me, and afterward we'd never have to speak of it again. Why else would she have called me, after all? I wanted to know the truth of the story, its truth and its meaning. I wanted to cast off my burden. And I was ready.

•

But she hadn't called to talk about the past. She didn't even refer to the past, much less clear things up the way I'd hoped, and my heart leapt with anticipation, crowed with joy, rose high over my head only to plummet back into the shadows, burrowing down in shame before the dawning truth that she was calling simply *to invite me to a party*—and will it never end, this continual pinching of the flesh in disbelief?—a "big party," to be precise. She was counting on me to come. It was important. She was asking as a favor, and she laughed faintly on her end while silently I kept telling myself that she had, in fact, called after all these years just to ask me to a party. As if nothing had happened and time had laid waste to everything and Michel Leiris were still alive.

•

Eyes closed, I listened. It was a birthday party for her husband's best friend, her husband who'd finally married her and was the father of her child, and every year Sophie—that was the friend's name, she was a "contemporary artist" (she said this in quotes), maybe I'd heard of her? Yes, exactly, Sophie Calle, the one who followed people in the street—anyway, every year this friend had a birthday party and invited as many people as she was years old plus a "mystery guest" who stood for the year she was about to live, and this year *she* was in charge of bringing the mysterious stranger and she couldn't say no, and so she'd thought of me (another faint laugh), and that was the reason, the one and only reason, for her call.

•

On my end I was stern. Galvanized steel. Clearly I was the one person she could think of who'd go along with this little charade of hers, and besides I made an ideal candidate seeing as how no one had ever heard of me. What's more, I thought, the mission must have actively appealed to her since, by picking up the phone just to invite me to a party, she'd overcome certain obvious objections raised by our history. She could hardly have acted in a spirit of pure disinterestedness, put it that way. But couldn't she have come up with a better pretext to see me—and did this mean she *wanted* to see me? Anything was possible. But why did she need a pretext? All she had to do was call and say "Let's get together" or even "We should get together" or better yet "Could we get together?" and if only she'd put it that way—any of these ways—she'd have acknowledged the ties that bound us, and always would, even if we were parted for hundreds of years, and then I'd have come running with a beating heart. But what did she mean by inviting me to a party? Who did she think I was? It was absurd, and I'd been kicked around enough, and yet I heard myself answer, in a voice that was almost chipper, that I'd be there. Consider it done, I told her. She could rest easy, I'd be her mystery guest, and all the while I gnashed my teeth with every fiber of my being. She sounded unaccountably relieved. No sooner had I spoken than her voice regained its scent of forget-me-nots, and I took down the time and address on a scrap of paper; then, without my knowing how it happened, she'd hung up. Not that we had anything left to say that could have been said on the phone.

•

My hand shook as I set down the receiver. The room was silent, the air livid, and the telephone sat chuckling on the bed until in my rage I lobbed it across the room; but it didn't even come apart, and for long seconds I lay there listening to the dial tone in the dark. And that was even worse than before. So I got up to put it where it belonged and hung it up, and I didn't know what to do, and I took a walk from one end of the apartment to the other, which didn't take long, and—that was the bouquet. No other words came to mind but "*C'est le bouquet.* This time, it's really the bouquet." For a good hour I paced the apartment repeating those words out loud as if they were the sum total of my vocabulary. All the same, the blood was fizzing in my veins: I couldn't deny feeling a thrill at the thought that I was finally about to have the meeting she'd owed me all these years. I was happy to make a fool of myself at some glamorous party. I'd gladly undergo much more painful transformations just to see her and finally hear her explain what she'd been thinking and cut the leash that bound me to her vanishing and put an end to this strangulation once and for all. I wanted answers. The rest of my life depended on that party, I knew that for a fact, and that night I dreamt of a horse trampling coattails in the dust.

II

The days and weeks that followed were unspeakable. Her call had plunged me back into a hellish slough that I'd considered well behind me, and that all of a sudden wasn't, and I fell back into sickening black thoughts I thought I'd exorcised, and was prey to grinning fiends, my old familiars, as if all my efforts to escape and move on had been worthless, as if nothing would ever come of anything. I felt like tearing the skin right off my face. For a long time I'd considered the case closed, as they say. I could go and buy bread at the bakery without thinking about her the entire time, and for this reason (and plenty of others) the affair seemed, as they say, laid to rest. I seemed to have turned the corner, as they say, and surfaced the way people tend to surface even if they come back utterly changed, wrecked, the change belied by a fold of the mouth, by something about their shoulders or hair, something unmistakable in the depths of their eyes, or the way they walk, or the way they laugh and talk and stand and—well, just look around you, you'll see what I mean.

•

Unless, as sometimes happens, the change is in the person's clothes. Since I'd always hated turtlenecks worn as undershirts and despised the men who wore them as the lowest kind of pseudo-sportsmen with, as they say, the lamest kind of collar, I started wearing turtlenecks as undershirts the moment she left. Basically, I never took them off. No doubt this was magical thinking on my part (if I never took them off, nothing would ever take off on me); at any rate, these turtleneck-undershirts erupted in my life without my noticing until it was too late and I was under their curse. You could even say they'd *inflicted* themselves on me, so that now I hardly remembered the wind on my neck, which is the very feeling of freedom itself. But if that was the price I had to pay, I told myself, so be it. We brick ourselves up in prisons of our own devising, we spend our lives losing touch with ourselves, disappearing behind what negates us. I took comfort in the thought that others had it even worse than I did, and I looked and saw people covered from head to toe in much more outlandish Band-Aids than my own. Yes, I told myself, my case was far from hopeless. In the end I'd found a workable way of moving incognito through the world and keeping up appearances, just like everybody else, and I moved freely, unbruised. Impunity was mine, and I was at peace. I'd even started seeing someone.

•

Yes, despite my turtleneck-undershirts a woman had taken an interest in me of late. And to my shock my turtlenecks didn't put her off, even though most women feel an instinctive, to my mind legitimate, revulsion toward men in layered turtlenecks, unless they somehow find them attractive—but I gave those women a wide berth then and still do. At any rate she wasn't one of them; she just seemed not to notice my sartorial neurosis, for which I was profoundly grateful. At the same time it frustrated me. I was unnerved that my turtleneck-undershirts didn't bother her, never even gave her pause, when it would have made me feel so much less burdened and alone, would have meant such a sharp rise in the value of her affections, if only I'd known that she loved me with open eyes. But no, she saw no secret meaning in my layered look, so there I was, misunderstood at her side, furious, divided, unfairly and hatefully demanding that she *adjust* to my turtlenecks when it was exactly her easy acceptance of them that had brought us together in the first place, and everything about us is so twisted and convoluted, and doesn't every windfall hide a trap?

•

It's the worst, I told her. The worst in the sense that I can never get free and I keep looking like the person I seem to be and never was and never had been and never *would* have been except by force, as they say, of circumstance. Meanwhile she fell into the habit of rubbing her right cheek as if she were always trying to rub away—what?—some kind of permanent irritant, a slap that kept on stinging and had left her dazed and dumb. But when I pointed out that she hadn't exactly been born with this gesture she laughed and shrugged and told me I was making a mountain out of a molehill, as they say, and she refused to see this cheek-rubbing as anything more than a harmless idiosyncrasy (even though she couldn't stop doing it), and I didn't press the point because I didn't want to spoil the evening or poison things and because, in any case, none of this would have happened if, years before, this other person hadn't just *left* without a word of explanation, etc., etc., and because, all things considered, I preferred to sleep in the afternoon when there was no one around, and because *she* found me that way and asked me to a "big party," and on walls all across the city large posters were announcing the opening of *Die Hard*, and I was in despair.

•

At the same time all the headlines in the newsstands were full of German reunification, and *Best* was featuring "The Cure: Reintegration" on its cover while *Guitar & Clavier* had "Rita Mitsouko Remixed." Poised on the eve of the third millennium, the times seemed to be in a frenzy to recycle the past so as to proceed that much more jauntily into the future and went scurrying around trying to settle accounts before opening any new ones. So,

I decided, her call might not have been an entirely random occurrence. It was part of the march of history and was, in a certain historical sense, more significant than I'd first understood. We *are* all products of our environment, after all. And this was one possible explanation, because, amid all the chaos of my feelings and sensations, I was still struggling to solve the riddle of her call. Yes, it was a riddle—it was an offense to reason! I simply couldn't understand where she'd found the nerve to call me. I couldn't wrap my head around it. Was she trying to *destroy* me? Was she bent on my complete and utter annihilation? Was the whole thing some kind of plot? But too much water had gone under the bridge, as they say, for her to come looking for revenge after all these years—and besides, as far as I could tell, she didn't *have* anything to revenge. So this line of reasoning wouldn't hold up. There had to be some other explanation, clearly she had access to the same basic sentiments as everyone else, and I couldn't see my way out of it, my head was one big wound, and I twisted my neck in my turtleneck-undershirts, this way and that, looking around for whatever it was I was missing, because there had to be a meaning to it all, there simply had to be, or else the jig, as they say, was up and civilization had ceased to be anything more than a colossal lie—and why bother pretending to believe the lie in the so-called civilized countries of the world? And at the end of one afternoon I paused on the curb while cars shot toward me down the boulevard.

•

But I'd gotten over her disappearance and no one was going to say her reappearance did me in. I refused to give up. I wanted to understand, and while I stood there clinging absurdly, instinctively to this desire—to understand—as my sole support and the last vestige of my humanity, it hit me. She'd called late on a Sunday afternoon and she'd left me in the middle of the afternoon, also on a Sunday. Coincidence? Hardly. From that moment on, I knew I couldn't possibly be dealing with a coincidence. I knew bigger things were afoot. I couldn't get over the symmetry of the thing, and actually the truth was plain enough to see: by calling me on that day of the week, at that hour of the day, she was trying to pick up the thread of our story at just the point where it had been snapped in two, as if to say that all the intervening years had lasted a matter of seconds. And this changed everything. Suddenly time meant nothing and there was nothing final about her disappearance either, so our love had never ceased to be—all the rest was straw in the wind—and this business about the party was a pretext, a lure. After all, if all she'd wanted to do was invite me to the party she'd have called on a Monday morning or a Wednesday night or possibly on a Saturday in the middle of the day, but never late on a Sunday afternoon. Miracles do occur between people who've been in love, we all know that, and deep down I was overjoyed, I quivered, and her call, which at the time had struck me as the last word in brutality, suddenly made a kind of clear and overwhelming sense; such are the loopholes that reality offers us from itself.

•

For once I wasn't cooking the data. Not this time. Appearances never deceive (I told myself), they are their own meanings and there's nothing to look for behind them, and I rejoiced, and the reasons for her call rose up more and more vividly and gloriously into view. And the thing was, the reasons had nothing to do with her! Because it wasn't as if *she* had decided to call late in the afternoon on a Sunday and send me a coded message. No one was that roundabout, I told myself. At least not that *pointlessly* roundabout. So there had to be something else—call it a force—a force seeking some means of self-expression, struggling to give me a sign, and unbeknownst to her this something had told her to pick up the phone and dial my number at that moment, of all moments, the meaning of which apparent coincidence only I could discern. Yes, I was convinced that this had to be the explanation: for reasons unknown to me, but which might have had something to do with the death of Michel Leiris, something in her clicked and, taking advantage of her need to find a "mystery guest," the force stole this chance to slip her hand into mine, to wave a handkerchief like a prisoner locked in a tower. The force trusted me to hear the call within her call, in spite of everything. How else could I explain her years of silence—that is, without positing a counterspell which had finally lifted the curse? How else could I explain her complete failure to allude to the past during our conversation, the way any normal person would have done?

This in itself proved she wasn't behaving normally, that some larger power was working its will through her. And no doubt the psychoanalysts would speak of the "unconscious," but I told myself this force was nothing more or less than our love. Above and beyond our personalities and every barrier that existed between us, our love lived on. It had a life of its own and transcended us—not that there had ever been anything merely terrestrial about it. I thought of how certain comets venture to the edges of the universe only to return periodically toward Earth: in the same way, I was sure, our love was orbiting back in our direction after all the years it had spent banished to a distant frozen past. Obviously it was about to pass even closer at the time of the party, which was set for Saturday, October 13, 1990, and now this cluster of multiples of three struck me as a propitious sign, albeit with hazards of its own—and no, I'm not making any of this up. My imagination is much too good for that.

•

Any last doubts I had melted away. I was going to the party. How could I not? Such an alignment of events could take eons to reproduce itself—might never, ever come again. And there was no mistaking the sign I'd been given, and I was desperate to hold our love in my arms one last time, to feel the dizzying force of it, so much larger than either of us. At the same time I jeered at my own idiocy—my insanity, too, but mostly my idiocy—and despised myself for riding off after trouble like some kind of dimestore Don Quixote. Just what did I think I was going to achieve? Despair has a force of its own, and out of my despair I'd created a universe in which I was the star, and I was about to see this universe for what it was. This party would be the death of all my illusions, it would tear me to shreds and cripple me for life. Didn't I see the trap I was blundering into? She was making a fool of me, a laughingstock, and no one cared because I was such a nobody, I had nothing to look forward to but disaster and humiliation and more bitterness. I was like that general Aoun, shouting defiance from the rooftops of Beirut long after anyone could see it was in ruins. But I stopped my ears against my own misgivings, in which the voices of my mother and father and grandparents and great-grandparents and all my ancestors in every generation since biblical times were mingled, warning me in vain again and again (while I stuck to my guns) that I shouldn't come crying to them when I was a wandering shade: I had a rendezvous, even if I didn't know just what I was rendezvousing with. Nothing else counted and nothing could change my mind or turn me around, not when the great mystery of her leaving was about to be unveiled. I'd always thought I must be missing something. After all, no one just takes off on another person, a person she's loved, without some very specific, in the end very particular reason of her own. No matter how unhappy she may be, a woman at least says *goodbye* when she leaves. There had to be more to the story, and I had to know what it was and, when I did, I, too, would be unmasked and the curse of the turtleneck-undershirts would be lifted.

•

All the same, I was feverish and uneasy and in a state of absolute heartache and helpless rage at the prospect of showing up at this party where I was clearly supposed to play the part of a sentimental curiosity, where I'd be a stuffed monkey—where I'd be a dwarf, a dwarf to be thrown as far as possible so as to beat some dwarf-throwing record the precise nature of which eluded me. And I thought of Flint, Michigan, where the local directors of General Motors organized a big party as a consolation for everyone laid off after the "outsourcing" of some plant, and on the grounds of the mansion overlooking the town they gave the laid-off workers money to play living statues and hold poses while cigar-smoking men in tuxedos squired around women in silk evening gowns who sipped flutes of California champagne, and I thought of Baudelaire cutting the Belgians to ribbons and of Rimbaud insulting the literary men of his time and of Thomas Bernhard and Artaud and Alfieri and of Paul mailing off his epistles, and it made me happy just to know they'd existed. Suddenly I felt less alone. I felt emboldened by their example, as if somehow I shared in their refusal to be debased, to be robbed of their souls and selves. When my own turn came I would rip the mask from the face of the age we lived in and its most visible spokesmen. Yes, I, too, wanted to bolt from the ranks of the assassins and all their cronies, and if I was going to be the "mystery guest," well, they had no idea just what a mystery guest I'd be! Because I was thirty years old and the time had

come for me to make my presence felt. And I didn't
see anything vain or vapid about this line of thinking. Far from it. Just when circumstances were
least favorable (I told myself), that was the moment I'd turn them to my advantage, when no one
was looking, and like a jack-in-the-box I'd spring
the first chance they gave me. The moment they
let down their guard I'd make them dance!

•

To say I was afraid would be an understatement.
As the day and the hour of the rendezvous (or the
Reckoning, as I'd come to call it in my darker
moods) drew near, I seemed to be running help-
lessly toward my doom. I felt my strength fail, I
wavered in my determination, and the certainty
that I was going to lay bare the "figure in the car-
pet" faded, so great was the task before me, a task
I'd have to perform all alone. At least Ulysses had
his son by his side and the swineherd Eumaeus and
Whats his name, that cowherd, and the old serving-
woman and most of all Athena, who helped him
beat the suitors and in the end get Penelope back.
As for me, I had nobody, I was going it alone, and
the opposite of courage isn't cowardice but dis-

couragement, at least that's the opposite in French. These thoughts gnawed at my nerves and innards night and day and I couldn't think what to do and I worked myself into a fever trying on one heroic pose after another until, after several days, I slipped grimly into the costume of the mystery guest, I tricked myself out in it as if in a grotesque suit of armor and daubed myself with that name; and in my calmer moments as I waited for reality to hand down its verdict I felt very tenderly toward her again. And I remembered Alceste, and how in Act Five he gives his hand to the fallen Célimène; but just then I'd think of the money Humbert Humbert gives Lolita when he finds her reduced to a sordid double of her mother, then I'd wind up thinking of the Consul's miserable death at the foot of his volcano once he wins back Yvonne—and I wondered what as-yet-unwritten reunion was waiting for me. What revelations? What cruelties? What downfall?

•

By now all my euphoria had vanished, and I was furious with myself all over again and dead set against the part I was supposed to play. Who did they think they were? More to the point, who did they think *I* was? I had a name, she couldn't take *that* away too. I had to protect myself; yes, there are limits to what a man can agree to suffer, and I couldn't always just sit there and let other people prey on me with their desires and all their obscure machinations. I was going to show them who I was. They'd see, the world would see—it would see and *then* some! In the first place, I wasn't about to show up empty-handed. Because it hadn't been lost on me that this was a birthday party, in fact I'd spent hours racking my brains to figure out what a "mystery guest" should bring a person he doesn't know, a person who is, what's more, a "contemporary artist," and, from what I could gather, a *"well-known* contemporary artist," and this made me even angrier and more resentful and set the bar that much higher, as they say. But I couldn't come up with a present, and I tore my hair out pacing the length of my bedroom for the thousandth time, and besides I had no money, I mean nothing: I was so broke I wore secondhand shoes from the flea market at Clignancourt—but what was I doing, thinking about money and shoes, when the situation vitiated the very *idea* of present-giving, and the connection it implied between two individuals, a connection that meant more than just handing over some object (as I said, gnashing my teeth)? Unless I was supposed to come up with the world's most transcendent present—the present that symbolized The Gift, independent of any particular recipient or giver. Maybe that was what this Sophie of hers expected of the "mystery guest": to arrive at the highest possible conception of presenthood. Could that be what she had in mind? And so I kept walking the streets and going up and down the avenues and looking in every storefront; but wherever I looked all I saw was merchandise and more merchandise and nothing of any value except the value assigned to each thing in its turn by society, and nowhere I looked did I see any object that seemed to incarnate anything more than profit and gain, and in every direction lay all the commodities of the world expressing nothing so much as a degraded idea of The Gift, an idea contrary and, in a word, hostile to the idea of The Gift rightly understood, and the last thing I wanted was to arrive at that party bearing a gift that would shed its mystique the moment the colored paper and ribbon had been torn aside. And all at once I saw why our societies use gift wrap: not for the sake of surprise but rather to cover up the fact that The Gift is based on a lie, as we inevitably discover every time somebody gives us something, yes, and we open it and, after that microsecond when we expect the fulfillment of our deepest desire, disgust and sadness wash over us and we smile as fast as we can and say thank you, the better to bury our chagrin at never once in all our lives receiving something more than what we'd hoped for. And this evanescent joy, forever disappointed, remains incomprehensible to us.

•

For a while I toyed with the idea of giving her a book by Michel Leiris. At least it beat flowers or candy, I told myself. It would be dull and anticlimactic, that went without saying, but it seemed like the least worst option I had—and, after all, haven't we spent years in default mode, in faute de mieux mode, following the path of least badness as if nothing nowadays merited our full and utter and joyful consent? And how long, I began to wonder, can this go on? How long can we go around economizing our desires? And that's when

I stopped short, right there in the middle of the street. *I'd give her wine!* It was so obvious I couldn't think why it hadn't occurred to me before. What could be better? My search was over, I'd bring her wine. A very good bottle of wine, the oldest and most expensive wine that money could buy. And this idea struck me as nothing short of brilliant, as if, coming from the depths of my being and my heritage, it battened on my energies and desires until it grew huge and glorious, until I could no longer contain it and burst out laughing, still standing right there in the street. Yes, if they wanted my blood, I thundered to myself, I'd give them vintage blood, and a very good vintage at that, and they would drink it in remembrance of me—and wasn't Christ himself a model mystery guest? The more I thought it over, the more dazzled I was by my plan. For once I'd come up with the perfect thing. And in a wine store near Saint-Lazare I found a 1964 Margaux. I remember it perfectly. It was the best bottle in the store, and it was way beyond my means, and I exulted, I actually pranced with delight in front of the clerk, who peered at me suspiciously and even looked a little bit nervous. But that was just it: I wanted to sacrifice everything, I wanted to shame them as I climbed up on the pyre. We'd see how haughty they looked then. We'd see whether they had brought anything beyond *their* means—in a word, I challenged them to a potlatch and for once I put all social chicanery aside, and they would know who'd really give all for love, and the bottle cost more than my rent, a lot more, and that didn't matter. On the contrary, I'd crossed the Rubicon, as they say. The so-called die had been cast, and the rent could wait. (Which in fact it did.) On my way out of the store, as I cradled my tissue-wrapped bottle to my chest like a talisman, the city seemed to have changed its aspect. It was all light farce, and I felt tall enough to cross outside the crosswalk. I could stop cars with a glance, I could contend with their bumpers and hulls, and I no longer had any fear that the distress and indigence of the world might rub off on me. No, never again would my own opulence be reduced to begging, I chanted to myself, for at that moment it seemed to me that I had earned the right to quote Hölderlin, a thing that doesn't happen every day.

•

How much had changed since her phone call! I'd been at loose ends and now I was on a mission. And I wasn't alone anymore, I contained multitudes, and I had to go, the hour was upon me. To hell with the expense, I told myself, hailing a cab to the party with no more thought for the future than a condemned man accepting his last cigarette. Leaning my head against the window, the bottle of '64 Margaux resting on my knees and my hands resting—brooding—on it all the way, I watched the lights and the shadows go by and I remembered how it all started with the death of Michel Leiris, and since then I'd been apprised, as they say, that hundreds of millions of Germans had been reunified and sung the "Ode to Joy" on the steps of the Reichstag, and riots had broken out in Vaulx-en-Velin, and in Rwanda rebels had overrun the north of the country, and an anthropologist had confirmed that social ties between baboons were based on affection, and the Bayeux tapestry might not really date from the eleventh century after all because they didn't start cooking with skewers until the 1700s, and an attack had left twenty dead in Jerusalem's Mosque Square while three mountain climbers had conquered Everest. And I'd jotted each of these items down in a little notebook so I could remember them later on, because that whole week I never lost the feeling that I was participating in world events and was linked, in a tiny invisible way, to everything that took place everywhere. And in the taxi I closed my eyes and tried to reconstruct the chain that had me in it as a link. But no matter how I tried, all I came up with was rioters using skewers in Jerusalem with baboons to the tune of the "Ode to Joy," or something equally beside the point, yes, despite my best efforts everything that had, as they say, transpired in that week's news kept adding up to a series of interchangeable words, just piles and piles of words, and reality struck me as an absurd fiction, terrifying in its absurdity—and wasn't that exactly the way it was presented in the first place? That's when I remembered the space probe *Ulysses*. It had been launched toward the Sun the previous day, or maybe the day before, and for the first time (if I understood correctly) a man-made object was going to leave Earth's orbit and break free of the gravitational pull of all the planets and leave the solar system. And this wasn't nothing. And, now that I was thinking about it, I actually found myself praying for the little probe to make it all the way. Here, finally, was an event that answered to my own experience. Here, finally, was a sign, something to give me hope instead of drilling my own disgust and helplessness into me and making me feel puny and afraid. And I felt peaceful and confident and, in a certain way, nourished by all the efforts of the most creative brains on the planet, and sitting there in the shadows I smiled down at the bottle of Margaux and made sure it wasn't getting bounced around in my lap. Then the driver ventured to say something about its being chilly for early October and how you couldn't predict the weather anymore. And I didn't much feel like talking, but there was no stopping him, he was in a confiding mood, and he told me that after his wife left him two years earlier he'd lost seventeen kilos. Seventeen kilos. He still couldn't believe it. And he chuckled in quiet alarm as if it haunted him even now; and I said maybe that's how much his wife weighed for him, seventeen kilos. He glanced at me in the rearview mirror. Clearly, he'd never seen it that way before. It had never occurred to him that love might not just feel like a burden, that it might also have an actual, physical weight. Then I let him in on the secret of my turtlenecks so he'd know we were in the same boat, but he seemed distinctly unimpressed and just nodded and turned up the radio in time to hear a voice introduce "the last recording of 'L'Aigle noir' by the immortal Barbara." And for the duration of the ride, which took forever, I couldn't stop thinking that the black eagle had come back, come back out of nowhere; and we all have our mystery guests; and the fare was ninety-two francs at the time.

She wasn't the one who answered the door. She did not appear before me as on the first day, sculpted in light, stepping out of the party. And we didn't stand there staring at each other in silence, moved beyond words, gazing hungrily after years of yearning while the old enchantment revived and twined itself around us and the same smile, beginning on her lips, moved to mine as if it were a kiss that had never ended. In real life nobody came to let me in. The place where the taxi dropped me off was gloomy, across from a railroad track with big concrete panels clearly designed to muffle the noise of the trains, and nothing made a sound but the streetlights, shining on a deserted corner, and in the cold they produced a uniquely tentative, peevish halo of light. I don't know how long I must have stood there, tapping my foot on the sidewalk, stuck and at a loss, facing the small bare metal door. Evidently it had been cut from the much larger door of a garage or old factory and there was no way to tell what was going on behind its iron or what would happen to me once I crossed the threshold. And I wanted to turn tail, as they say, and run away in search of a better, less arduous life. I had nothing to do with this neighborhood, I told myself. Nothing here made any sense at all. Even the intercom was forbidding, and it took me several minutes to figure out that I had to scroll down a list of names to find, displayed on a little greenish screen, the name Sophie Calle. In the end nothing was turning out the way I'd imagined—not that I'd formed any precise idea of what awaited me when I got there. But in any case it wasn't really all that cold for the time of year, and my fingers weren't stiff from clutching the bottle of Margaux, and what did intercoms and streetlights matter? It's just that in my mind I'd arrived at the party and there I'd *been*, in medias res, as they say, and no contingency, no sharp peaks or ridges held me back. But this was not the way things were tending. On the contrary. And suddenly I felt disillusioned with all the ideas and pinwheels and roman candles that had been sparkling inside me all week, and it was as if the weight of things came and took me by the hand, looking to sully me with their banality. And I just knew, at that moment the probe *Ulysses* was dealing with some serious turbulence of its own. But it hardly made sense to turn around now. The time for second guesses and deliberation had passed, however you looked at it, and soon enough (I told myself with wry detachment) I'd know whether I ought to have given up or gone through with it, and I screwed up my courage, as they say, and I took a deep breath and solemnly, so solemnly it actually made me smile, pressed the intercom. But nothing came out. No buzzer buzzed. No echo greeted this act which, it seemed, set nothing in motion, as if nothing had taken place, as if—in a word—I did not exist. And for a fraction of a second the world flickered before my eyes and grew dark. How could there only be silence when everything within me cried out that I'd done something tremendous? There had to be some mistake; reality could not depart so utterly from what I felt. Could the world really be so perverse as to call into question the simple fact of my having rung a doorbell? It couldn't be *that* demonic. And I pushed the button again, hoping desperately that something somewhere was buzzing and that someone was going to hear it, and it crossed my mind that a century before no one could have imagined a human being reduced to such a strange and wonderful hope; but still nothing happened, the silence was unbroken, and I began to count the seconds (not noticing that they were actually the sound of my racing heart) while my eyes lingered on the white paint peeling around the edges of the intercom, and for a brief instant I found myself absorbed in the forms born of this degradation, recognizing here the body of a woman with a hat, there a face in profile, until eventually they were starting to look more like clouds—when all at once the lock clicked in the door with a flat electric sound and the next thing I knew, guided by voices that grew ever more distinct, I crossed a small vegetable patch toward what seemed to be a disused factory, now converted into an artist's studio and, through the bay window that stretched across its façade, I saw that the party was, as they say, in full swing. And through the glass, from far away, I recognized her silhouette; so, of the two of us, I saw her first.

•

For there she was. She was standing with two men, one of whom was laughing, and a smile crossed her own lips, and she hid her mouth with her hand the way I'd always seen her do. This came back to me. And her hair was still as blond as I remembered, but shorter now. Or she was wearing it differently, I couldn't think which, and if I'd expected to feel overwhelmed, I didn't. I couldn't feel anything, really. The ground stayed put beneath my feet. In fact it was oddly familiar to have her there in front of me, familiar but in-congruous, and I pushed open the French door, careful not to bump the bottle of Margaux. Seeing me come in from the cold, a woman turned and smiled at me, and I smiled back and happened to notice the shape of her small breasts and, from that moment on, everything unfolded as if some-body else were acting in my place. That's how it felt. As if by entering the room I had also entered into a character, someone who hadn't been there a second ago, someone who took up the baton and composed my facial expressions so as to ward off any scrutinizing glances, someone who'd keep me from looking ridiculous, on the one hand, but also from making a scene or doing anything untoward. I wouldn't be allowed so much as a faux pas. I had been changed, despite myself, for better and for worse. It was as if I had no continuous inner life, whatever I might have thought, and I cursed my own sense of decorum. What was I waiting for? Well, I told myself, let them make one false move and all bets were off, I'd detonate their little charade. The game, as they say, wasn't over. In the meantime I took off my coat with the air of a man who knows how to take off his coat wherever he happens to be and rolled it up into a ball and stuck it next to a huge bunch of red and white roses. They were spilling out of a vase that had been planted on the floor, and it crossed my mind that this bouquet took up an inordinate amount of space, maybe not quite as much as the *Odyssey* in my life, but almost. And despite myself I started to count the roses. All of a sudden it seemed absolutely necessary that I find out, then and there, how many roses were in the vase, so that at least some part of my surroundings wouldn't remain unknown to me, since sometimes just knowing *something* is enough to lull you into believing that you *know* something, and it turned out there were thirty-seven roses, and this had to be the number of candles that would later be blown out. And at the prospect of seeing a cake brought in and people singing "Happy Birthday" I felt defeated before the fact.

•

No one paid any attention to me and everything happened exactly the way it always does: enigmatically, without your being able to put your finger on the enigma. And I lit a cigarette to keep my hands and lungs and all the rest busy while, with an air of unconcern, as they say, I threw myself into the fray, sure that everyone had already noticed my turtleneck. Without meeting anybody's eye I marched straight ahead and cleared a path as if I knew exactly where to go and how to get there, and it worked: underneath a big iron staircase that led to the upper floor I found a place where I could observe things from out of the way, without anyone slipping behind me, and just then

I felt the hardest part was over, so I looked up and took in the proceedings.

•

The room was enormous. From the center a table advanced endlessly toward the walls, spreading itself with mile after mile of silver, and a dazzling white tablecloth made up of several sheets lay like a bridal train under the bright track lights up above, and chairs and stools were drawn up all around it. At the foot of the stairs a stuffed cat was pouncing without ever touching down on its forepaws, and farther off stood a pink flamingo on one leg, and the atmosphere was cheerful. It was festive. Everywhere men and women discussed and conversed and were generally moving around, and some went and others came, and many of the guests wore black and smoked, and some were sitting and had their elbows on the table and picked at saucers holding little canapés or slices of dried sausage, and most were drinking champagne, and one woman was insisting that they put on some Spanish music while over in the corner a man in a white panama hat seemed to be in some kind of sulk. In other words, it was a party, there was no doubt about it, it was a party like any good party, and in a sense this was reassuring. All the same, I fought back an urge to howl while I beamed a perfectly fake smile back and forth at no one in particular. At some point a woman carrying a large platter toward the table slipped and fell, and this piece of slapstick drew people's attention, heads turned, and that's when she saw me. Her gaze crossed the room and landed where I was, and she interrupted the man who'd been laughing, she laid a hand on his arm and murmured something in his ear, and the man glanced up in my direction while she moved away from him and came toward me. And the way his eyes followed her from behind kept me from enjoying this moment which I'd promised myself as recompense. Yes, it spoiled everything, but no more than everything else did in the end. And I stood there, stock-still with a frozen smile the whole time I watched her coming nearer. And she was very beautiful, I had forgotten just how beautiful she was, and at the same time I didn't remember her having been beautiful in quite this way, or ever having worn this dress. It bared her shoulders and made her instantly desirable and, so to speak, sexual. So sexual that, as she passed, all the men and the women, too, caressed her with their eyes, and thousands of feelings and impressions came washing over me, all of them tending toward the question of whether she'd chosen this dress for my sake, to seduce me—to bring me, as they say, to my knees—or else to show me that we moved in different worlds now and she belonged to somebody else. Not that the two scenarios were mutually exclusive. Maybe she wanted to exercise her powers of seduction over everyone and no one. And I do know it goes without saying that a woman never chooses her clothes at random, at least not in a situation such as this. But whatever secret motives had gone into choosing her outfit, I couldn't sort them out in the folds of her dress, they all kept jangling together in my mind. The mere act of keeping myself in one piece seemed like a kind of magic trick, and I felt a trap door give way beneath my feet when she came up and leaned in to kiss my cheek as if it were the most natural thing in the world. But this really was the final straw. How dare she? It wasn't just inappropriate, it was obscene, it was phony through and through, as if our story could ever, even conceivably, degenerate into—into what? Friendship? Camaraderie? Whatever she had in mind, it was out of the question! She could save these affectations, these empty shams of hers for other men, or else love meant nothing and our story had never happened and she herself didn't exist, and just then I could have torn her face off, I could have ripped it from her neck and stamped on it before she uttered a word. How was I supposed to accept it that what had bound us together, and still *did* despite everything, should moulder away into anything as reasonable and pitiful as a kiss on the cheek, into something that had nothing to do with us? We deserved better and she knew it, and *inoffensive* was the last word you could ever use to describe our story, and what begins in beauty, as they say, can only end in beauty— otherwise what was the point of Michel Leiris dying in the first place and what was the point of inviting me to this party? But maybe all she wanted was to catch a whiff of my scent after all these years and relive, for an instant, the touch of her skin against mine without laying herself open to reproach. It was true that her attitude gave me some cause for hope. In any case, it was too late.

I'd already kissed her cheek, closing my eyes and clenching my fists and fighting the urge to seek her lips and find and open them and taste her tongue and lose myself there the way I used to do—and so to put an end to this charade I placed the bottle in her hands, saying, "From the mystery guest." And I hope no one ever has to smile the way I smiled then.

•

I have no memory of what we said, none at all, since in that moment all I could listen to was her face. I couldn't get beyond what it was telling me, because everything was written in her cheeks, her cheeks which she'd lost, which had melted away and were gone, and it was as if the last vestige of her childhood had vanished and left something burnt, something *consumed* in its place—there was no other word to describe it, and this was so intolerable that it actually hurt to look her in the face. I couldn't help feeling sorry and on the verge of tears, and all at once I realized how much she must have gone through, how much she had to have endured, and I turned my face away to keep her from reading the sadness in my eyes, which was bigger than any sadness of our own. And I thought she must have noticed certain things about me, too, which she was keeping to herself and which couldn't have been all that pretty, either—and could it be that every second of this party would be a trial and an affront and a calvary of endless disillusionment? Because now she'd seized the bottle of Margaux and gripped it by the neck, and I wanted to let this detail go but she was clutching it and waving it around, she was *gesticulating* with it, and inside I was groaning in shock. Yes, at that moment I'd have given anything for her to intuit that she was holding in her hands not just a bottle of wine, and of a very grand cru, but, underneath all that tissue paper, something like my soul, in any case the best I had to offer and, in a word, the token of what had been invited mysteriously into our lives and changed them forever. But no, she manhandled the bottle as if it were just anything, and I felt as though I were the one swinging in the air, yet again, without a word of explanation, as though in the end we'd never stood a chance and no man and woman ever stood a chance, and I didn't want to know or think about it anymore, she'd floored me, we were still in Round One of the party and I was already down, as they say, for the count. I distinctly felt some part of me detach

itself and flit off across the room and disappear
through the bay window, and for long seconds all I
could do was gaze out over the people who revolved
and surged around us, singling out now a woman's
tousled hair, now the flame struck from a lighter,
now a slice of toast on a plate, and the stuffed cat
was still springing under its chair and the man
with the panama hat had gone off someplace, and
finally I looked back at her and she was speaking
to me through a sort of fog, and her shoulders
were bare, and her slight breasts rose toward me
against the material of her dress, and I had no
business being there, I should never have come,
and my whole life was going to be a nightmarish
lipogram in which, as the missing character, she
would never appear.

•

Maybe there was no more to say than our eyes
had already taken in. Now we both fell silent, with
no words to bridge the time and space between
us when, just then, she stopped a woman walking past. "Sophie," she burst out, "your mystery
guest." At this the woman looked up at me. She
had a broad, open smile, and a lock of hair had

come loose over her forehead. There was something almost girlish about her excitement. She
didn't seem to know which way to turn, and just
then nothing could have struck me as stranger or
harder to grasp or, in the end, more grating than
this euphoric enthusiasm. It was more than I could
take, and I gave her what I hoped was a blank, her-
metic stare. I had no intention of playing the good
little mystery guest. No, I'd sworn to be myself, to
give no ground to this amusement of theirs, which,
as far as I was concerned and in my current state of
mind, wasn't the least bit funny—as if what they
call society wasn't already engaged in a ceaseless,
unremitting, all-out, often very *amusing* campaign
to destroy every trace of our personalities. Why
should I go out of my way for her? I wouldn't lift
my little finger, as they say; at the same time I felt
bovine and oafish and stupid and scarlet, and just
to keep from standing there mute until something
really unforgettable popped out, I wished her a
happy birthday, and she thanked me and took the
bottle of 1964 Margaux in her arms. And I wished
she'd tear off the tissue paper then and there and
show the world what I'd done. I wanted her to go

into ecstasies over my present. Instead she waved hello to someone who must have just walked in, then she turned back and gave me a good long look and playfully asked who I was. And maybe she wasn't just being playful, because she watched me closely, as if she were somehow on the catch and crouched in wait, and I racked my brain for something to say that wouldn't sound utterly foolish. I felt stupid and guilty and inadequate all at once, and after a long silence I croaked that I was currently an expert in the cruelties of existence. And I glared at her defiantly (I was actually trying to stare her down), past caring whether I looked like a moron or not. My attitude didn't seem to faze her in the least. On the contrary, she kept looking into my face and smiling and her eyes crinkled and if anything I seemed to have amused her and piqued her interest, and without meaning to we held each other's gaze. And for a fraction of a second there was a spark between us, then just as quickly it died away, and she had opened her mouth to speak when an arm reached out and grabbed her and a woman with blood-red lipstick shouted right in her ear that they needed her in the kitchen. They were having an emergency, a disaster involving the oysters—or something, I don't remember what, and she seemed apologetic, and she gave me a meaningful glance, though I couldn't have said what it was supposed to mean, while she let herself be led away toward the kitchen, and just then I realized that she was disappearing with the bottle of Margaux and it was all I could do not to yell out and run after her. It was my bottle, and nobody was going to open it and drink it without my permission, and next to me the person who was the whole reason for the evening's show-and-tell just stood there not doing anything, and I gasped to her that I'd brought a grand cru and that I really hoped we could raise a toast with it together. That's all I wanted, to raise a toast, *"à nos amours,"* as they say—and that was when she informed me that her friend never opened the presents she got for her birthday. At first I refused to believe it. I dismissed it out of hand. The basic mistakenness of my being there could only go so far, and everything has a limit, so naturally I assumed she was joking just to scare me and rob me of the last shred of my dignity. But she was serious, and she explained that for several years Sophie had kept her birthday presents unopened in display cases that she photographed afterward, and the idea was to turn them into an exhibition someday, or maybe a book, she wasn't sure which; at any rate it was a kind of ritual, and she guessed she should have warned me when she called but it slipped her mind, and why should it have occurred to her, and it was hardly the end of the world, all we were talking about was a bottle of wine, and I nodded and looked straight ahead, seeing nothing but the wall, the wall that kept rising and rising around me and now towered over me near completion, and I couldn't stop nodding my head like one of those plastic dogs in the backs of cars, and I knew that it was my fate to be misunderstood and nothing I'd done had ever been any use or served any purpose, and what on earth did I care about contemporary art? I didn't! I couldn't have cared less! And I wanted to burst out laughing, I wanted to laugh until my jaw came unhinged and my teeth and eyes and bones fell apart and I disintegrated into atoms and disappeared, never to be heard from again.

•

I went out into the garden to get some air, and the cold did me good. For a long time I just stood there, filling my lungs and breathing out steam and looking up at the stars, and way up there the little probe *Ulysses* must have been spinning away at thousands of kilometers per second, making its way across the solar system. Even at that speed it would take years to reach the Sun, and I thought that in the end it was a kind of mystery guest in the galaxy. The little probe never gave up, and it faced perils considerably more daunting than anything strewn along my path, and through the bay window I looked around for her, and she was in the midst of a conversation with the man who'd made her laugh before, and he had to be the one she lived with, it was clear from the way he touched her arm—and was that what she wanted to show me by bringing me here? Her new life? Her happiness? Her unhappiness? I didn't understand. I'd missed something, and I needed to know what it was. I'd come too far, now I couldn't give up. No, how could I face the next few hours all alone with the image of a cat frozen solid, halfway pounced? The idea seemed worse and worse. And I pushed open the French door, and the hubbub and warmth of the party swept over me again, and I found myself wanting a drink. I found myself wanting several drinks. And I headed in the direction of the table, quickly checking to make sure my coat was still there because I was seized by the fear that somebody might have stolen it, or that it might have been vaporized, and I had to reassure myself that nothing of the sort had taken place, and this couldn't wait, nothing else mattered just then, and in the end we never dread anything that hasn't already come invisibly to pass, and next to my coat the bouquet of white and red roses seemed to be giving off signals, trying to tell me something, and it seemed like the only solid and benevolent thing at the party.

•

Back at my observation post under the stairs I was busy downing one glass of champagne after another, waiting for something to intervene and save me, waiting and willing the pink flamingo to put down its other leg, when a woman with complicated earrings that dangled down almost to her shoulders came up to me and made as if to toast. And although I didn't have much to say, and didn't feel like talking, I couldn't just leave her there in front of me like a puddle, so I asked her who all these people were having such a good time all around us. And she started pointing out faces and naming names and most of them were people I'd heard of, some were actually famous, and there were artists and writers and intellectuals and journalists, there was even a star bullfighter, and I told her it was funny, none of these celebrities really *looked* very much like celebrities to me. To me they looked more like little bits of bread bobbing around and sinking in a bowl of milk. I got the feeling I'd said, as they say, the wrong thing: she stiffened slightly and replied in a strained voice, eyeing my glass, that I was the one who should probably switch to milk. Her earrings tinkled their disapproval, and I was abashed and bowed my head, and at the same time, it was too late, something shot out of me, something bounded and tore through my mouth, twisting it up while I stood there helpless, and before I knew what was going on I was letting her have it, telling her that we had a little problem on our hands, it seemed to me, yes, here we had all these beautiful people making their beautiful things, standing up for even more beautiful things—and, she shouldn't get me wrong, it was all to the good, it was beautiful, but could she name me one celebrity in that room, just one, who could truly and in good conscience claim to be *over and above* it all? Because that I would love to see. Really, I'd be curious to see that. And she might recall that people used to use that expression, "over and above," and not all that long ago, either, and was it really any wonder if the expression had fallen into disuse, if it had actually disappeared from the general vocabulary, if in point of fact nobody said it anymore, or *could* honestly say that he or she was over and above when, along with the expression, what we'd lost was the very possibility of truly *being* over and above, even of dreaming of being over and above, when this desire couldn't even be put into words anymore, and [I didn't really know where I was going with this] could we be absolutely sure that these people would be famous in any other world but this one, or even that they'd exist? Because if we couldn't be sure of *that*, then what good were their works and all their renown—and there was no need to look at me like that, she could just keep her looks to herself, because in case she was interested in hearing how *I* felt, how I felt around these people, I felt like the kind of person nobody ever wants to hear anything out of and then all they do is tell them that they're wrong and don't understand anything and are worthless and ought to just keep their mouths shut and all they are is some surprise guest that they put up with at the table of life— and *what*, I wanted to know, did she think of *that*? She didn't think much of it, evidently, and no sooner had I ended this tirade than I began to regret having opened my mouth. There was no point attacking her. After all, she hadn't been invited to the party by accident. She couldn't possibly understand what I was saying. And I was ashamed, and at the same time I was relieved. Yes, I was ashamed for no discernible reason and I was relieved for no discernible reason, and after a few long seconds, during which she treated me to her profile and the swaying of an earring, which she absentmindedly fingered, she turned and stared at me as though I'd just become an enemy, a personal enemy, and asked whether I happened ever to have published a book, whether I'd ever published anything at all. And I felt myself blush and confessed I hadn't and her face relaxed and she gave a little smile, as if everything had just clicked into place. As if all of a sudden everything made sense. She saw where I was coming from, and my own insignificance explained all the nonsense I'd been spewing, and she said just what I expected her to say, that it was easy and comfortable to criticize people who created things because at least they took risks. At least they tried. And I was about to put up an argument, but deep down I agreed and kept quiet while she told me, in a ringing voice, that she'd rather talk to someone with talent and manners. And I saw her point, I told her, as she turned on her heels and clicked her earrings, and I raised my glass to her back as she moved away. And I was furious with myself, and it was a good thing we'd never gotten married, and we never stop clinging to the idea that things could always be worse. When I was little, wasn't that just what they used to tell me to quiet me down? And just then nothing struck me as more absurd—worse than absurd: toxic, mortifying—than to remain the way I was, good and quiet and seen and not heard, as they say.

•

But why didn't *she* come and talk to me? Now she was deep in conversation with another couple and seemed to have forgotten all about me, and I'd had enough of this mincing around, I'd had enough

period, and, for starters, I'd had enough of standing there under my staircase. So, in order to save
face and give myself a manageable goal, for once,
I made up my mind to go stand next to the bay
window and get another view of the party, thinking maybe over there I'd see things, things like my
life and the world, in another light. Sometimes, I
thought, all it takes is a slight adjustment. And it
was a step in the right direction, if nothing else,
and at any rate I'd come to a decision, and not a
minute too soon. At the same time I was looking
around for our hostess. I wanted to avoid her at all
costs. I wanted to keep from bumping into her since
I felt completely incapable of saying anything that
wasn't fraught with distress and indigence. Yes, it
was better for everyone, myself included, if I kept
my own counsel for the time being. Much better.
And finally I rounded a pillar and there to my surprise stood the man in the panama hat, and he
turned on me, staring with burning blue eyes.
They were the palest blue you can imagine. His
face was strangely smooth and flat and at the same
time deeply etched, and he took my hand and said
hello in a soft, inaudible voice. And I shook his
hand, and it was like his voice, and I gave him

what I hoped was my friendliest smile, as if I were afraid of hurting him. Because he seemed somehow fragile, something about him seemed to be crying out for help, and I was going to take back my hand but instead of letting go he squeezed and clutched it and—what was going on? Suddenly he staggered and tipped over backward as if he were in the grip of some kind of seizure, but I couldn't tell what it was. The life went out of his body, and he seemed to be melting away right where he stood, and I saw him fall back, and he wasn't fighting it, in fact he seemed to be letting it happen, and I thought he was going to collapse in front of me, and at the thought that he might really be sick I panicked, and now I was the one clinging to his hand. I wanted to keep him from falling down, I wanted to avoid that more than anything, but it was all happening too fast and he was convulsing right there where we were standing, and I couldn't think what to do, when my eyes met his and I realized that there wasn't anything wrong with him at all. I knew this kind of glance. And something in me froze and without flinching I faced down his desire, and he must have been able to tell he'd lost me, because he closed his eyes as if he were privately savoring some final regret, then slowly he opened them and I asked in the harshest, most sarcastic tone I could muster whether he was feeling any better; but he didn't look up, and I heard him murmur with a sigh, "You are very handsome." And I nodded at him, my jaw clenching uncontrollably, and I let go of his hand. And he made no effort to hold on to mine, the wave had subsided, and once more his eyes were bottomless and brimming over with something unpleasant and sour. And without another glance in my direction he moved away, limping slightly, and while I gazed after him something rose up in me, part disgust, part fear, and part humiliation. This whole episode couldn't have lasted more than a couple of seconds, and no one had seen it happen, and later I learned that the man was Hervé Guibert. And that was the first writer I'd ever met, as they say, in the flesh, and what good did it do to read so many books (I gnashed) if that's what things came down to? And for a long time I just stood there, feeling like a gob of spit, and now it was settled, no matter what might happen to me here, no good could come of it or make me feel better or calmer. I'd only feel diminished and ugly and vain and artistic and French and refuted, once and for all. Refuted from head to toe.

•

But later in the party a slight woman with brown hair who must have been awfully pretty once, and in fact still was, told me that she crossed the cemetery at Montparnasse every afternoon on her way home from work and always made a detour to steal the flowers from Pierre Laval's tomb and bring them home with her. And her house was always full of flowers because every day more flowers appeared on Pierre Laval's tomb, astonishing as that seemed, and as she put it no flower deserved to die on such a tomb, and she considered it a kind of mission to save them. And her eyes glittered with malice and I excused myself to make a call and she pointed me toward the phone, and so when I called the woman who loved me despite my turtleneck-undershirts (I'd promised to call and reassure her), I told her I was having a great time. There was nothing for her to worry about, I was holding up just fine and wouldn't stay much longer, and I'd tell her all about it in the morning. And I told her I was thinking of her, and at that instant it was truer than it had ever been, even as my eyes followed the path of a young woman in an orange bolero whose figure had already made an impression on me even in the midst of all these distractions and contortions, in their midst or else because of them, and I couldn't have explained exactly what I wanted with her, maybe just to hear her voice or speak to her or come up behind her and run my hands under her bolero and feel her skin and englobe her breasts and fondle them and knead them without her minding or being aroused or even startled. On the contrary, she would close her eyes in abandon and let herself be flooded by the sensation, and everything would be simple and self-evident and glowing orange—and wasn't I, after all, a guest of all the mysteries?

•

She was studying psych, as she put it, and while we stood there in the kitchen I kept up a steady stream of talk, as best I could, just to keep the curve of her lips there before me and her delicate wrists and her throat, her throat that seemed to call out for strangulation. And I didn't quite understand how our conversation wound up where it did, but she had just been describing the Lashley experiment, and I didn't know what that was, and she was explaining how they took rats and trained them to feed from a green trough and gave them an electric shock if they tried to eat out of a red trough, and the rats became neurotic, and so far so good, I followed what she was saying. But then they got rid of the green trough and the rats only had the red trough to eat from, knowing all the while that they'd get electrocuted if they went near it, and you can imagine the conflict, she told me, her eyes shining (and I certainly could), and in the end the rats go crazy: they start turning around in circles for hours on end or they become violent and aggressive for no apparent reason. And some of them devour their own extremities or throw themselves against the sides of their tank until they lose consciousness, and after several days most of them stop moving and end up immobile and prostrate, and they get into this mental *fog*, and then you can make them hold any kind of pose, no matter how ridiculous or uncomfortable, without their showing the slightest reaction. And I drained my glass and told her that for many of us the moment when they got rid of the green trough had already come, it seemed to me. Maybe for all of

us. All you had to do was look around you and wherever you looked you'd find people contorting themselves in unlifelike ways in a mental fog. And
couldn't you get the basic idea just by turning on
the evening news and peering into the mental fog
of its unlifelike presentation of everything unlifelike and mentally foggy that took place in the world
every day? And the thought bore down on me that
my way of being and of doing things, even my way
of writing, was equally absurd and foggy, and I was
seized by a kind of panic, I felt myself break into a
sweat, my turtleneck was choking me and clinging
to my skin and frantically I started looking around,
trying to find a way out. There had to be a way out
or I couldn't go on. But I didn't see a way out, because there was none, and I looked at her and I could
see her wondering what was the matter, and all at
once I conjured her lips, her wrists, her neck, her
bolero, and suddenly something in me relaxed, and
the air and the blood and the life rushed back in.
And in a stronger voice, a voice that was almost in-
souciant and betrayed nothing of the little tour of
nothingness I'd just taken, I told her it was lucky she
was wearing an orange bolero, not a red one. Really,
she had no idea how lucky it was at that particular

moment. It held out hope for the rest of us. And I didn't have anything in mind—not the way she must have thought, because she gave me a tight smile, only pretending to be put out when I said I'd bored her long enough and the pleasure had been all mine and I'd learned something new. In fact she'd opened my eyes, and that was enough in itself.

•

We'd spent the party crossing paths and playing a kind of elaborate hide-and-seek and she hadn't once come up to me with any intention of referring to the past. Much less to say she was sorry, although I'd have been satisfied with that, yes, I'd have been satisfied just to hear her say she was sorry. Even if she hadn't referred to the past I'd have known what she meant. Just *I'm sorry*. And maybe she could have taken my hand for one brief second and squeezed it. Yes, I'd have been content just to feel the pressure of her fingers. I wasn't asking anything more than that. But she never once budged from beginning to end, she stood aloof, and maybe she hadn't found the nerve, or the right moment, or the inclination, I didn't know, and it had stopped mattering. It was too late, the game was up. All the same, I did try to slip a foot in the door that had stood closed between us all these years: we were standing near the bay window and she'd stopped to show me some photos of her daughter when I asked her with an air of unconcern, as they say, whether she'd heard about Michel Leiris. She had heard the news, she told me, but she'd never read him. Was he any good? I shrugged. It wasn't the moment to talk about literature. It wasn't the moment at all. And yet this answered the question. The death of Michel Leiris hadn't unlocked anything inside her. There'd been no connection in her mind between his disappearance and hers. It hadn't inspired her to call me, the way I'd thought, and this meant I'd come up with the metaphor all by myself to lend depth and meaning to her call and find some echo, out there in the universe, of the repercussion Leiris had made in me. And now it was time for me to go, as fast as I could, yes, I couldn't bear to spend another second in that room, among those people. Suddenly I was afraid of doing— what?—something I didn't want to contemplate, if everything went on the way it was, normal and innocent and insidious and perfect and underneath despairing and phony (these were the words

I was looking for), and I decided that things could just go on forever without a word of explanation, and so could I. In this, we were not alone. And my coat was where I'd left it, and in that sense, at least, all was not lost. And leaning down to pick it up I looked at my hands and turned them palms up and I seemed to see my life running through my fingers like a thin rain of sand, and none of it mattered at all.

•

Snatching my coat from the floor, where it lay balled up in its corner like a sleeping obedient dog, I glanced over at the bouquet of red and white roses, which really was magnificent and even, just then, unexpectedly beautiful. And despite myself I let the vision of them overwhelm and suffuse me. Each flower seemed to have been placed in such a way that a tacit, spontaneous line united them all, and the whole arrangement expressed a harmony that exalted no one flower in particular, a harmony that included even the least of them, yes, each rose seemed to blossom according to its own potential and at the same time took part in the larger design, leading me to reflect that who-ever had arranged those roses probably cherished certain socialist utopian ideals and had tried to express them in a vase of water, and that this might be all we could do—when I felt her come up behind me. She must have seen that I was leaving, vacating the premises, as they say—taking, as they say, French leave—and that now it was my turn to pack up and go without saying goodbye. I hadn't seen her walk over, but I knew it was her. And I didn't move. I wanted to spend one more moment contemplating the restful and, to tell the truth, nostalgic ocean of red and white petals before I faced this immense defeat of ours, this defeat that I knew would rise up endlessly before me once I'd crossed through the French doors. And suddenly I wasn't in such a hurry after all, and to gain time and put off the moment of straightening up and facing her, when everything would be over, I said quietly, "It really is a lovely bouquet, isn't it?" And I felt myself trying to sum up our story in those twelve syllables since I had the last word, which seemed fitting and necessary, and all at once I felt as though I was staging a scene and playing myself and my emotions, as if the best I could do was mime what I felt and act it out according to the safe laws of fiction. As if I didn't exist except in this effort at playacting, as if what I felt was neither here nor there, since I had no access to my actual feelings except as an idea, a pat, simplistic, conventional, credible, ready-made idea, a cultural commonplace. And this last inner renunciation of what I was going through was the hardest blow of all, and it was too late, it was all I could do just to make myself sound believable to her. And I stood there, not saying anything, knowing full well that these few seconds of silence created between us a "painful intensity" and an "ineffable emotion" and that, in a situation like ours, this was the thing to do: stop time so we could pretend to be in the presence of something inexpressible, which might stand for all the buried sadness of the world. And, after a while, it sort of seemed true. Even though I knew that this contrived, artificial silence was nothing but a big cliché, I couldn't help playing along and getting swept up in it, and all of a sudden I felt moved and sincere and close to her in a way I hadn't felt since she'd called and I'd seen her again. Yes, suddenly it began to seem as though our separateness was bringing us back together, managing the impossible while we stood in front of that bouquet, in that

silence. And during those freighted seconds everything grew more and more beautiful and harmo-
nious and red and white and orange between us,
and I wanted to believe in it, and I thought of us
looking in the same direction at that moment, for
what I knew would be the last time, and to end on
that note, as they say, seemed fair enough as memories go. So with my coat in my arms I stood and
looked at her, wanting to burn one last image of her
onto my heart, and her eyes were fixed on the bouquet, and without looking up, hardly moving her
lips, she murmured that roses were the only flowers she could bear to see cut, and immediately I felt
all the misapprehension that, to that moment, had
characterized my presence at the party drop away.

•

It was her tone of voice. There was something un-
placeable about it, something spontaneous, a kind
of aura that I didn't recognize. It was almost a
presence of its own. And for whatever reason it
startled me. Suddenly I tensed, my pulse quick-
ened, and I came to life. I fastened on her words
as if something, a hand maybe, had tapped me on
the shoulder or reached out and pinched me. And
her voice sounded so foreign and peculiar that at

first I thought someone else had spoken. At the same time I knew it was her. And this sensation hardly lasted half a second but it left me tingling with disbelief. She was oblivious to all this, completely oblivious. I looked and her face gave nothing away. The moment had passed and seemed never to have taken place, and she gazed at me with the same smooth, unfailing affability that she'd worn like a cloak throughout the party, and now I had no idea what to think. Still I felt—I knew for a fact—that her words hadn't come out of nowhere. I knew her little phrase meant something and that she'd said it for a reason. To tell the truth, I sensed that it had been (there is no other way to say it) a slip of the tongue, and in a rush it came to me that she'd sent me a message from deep within her. She'd given me a sign, yes, when I least expected it, just when I didn't see it coming, she'd betrayed herself in some way or another. Something had broken free inside her and stepped toward me naked, had stripped itself naked, in a word, and had spoken to me, had addressed me just when I'd given up all hope. And this time, I decided, she couldn't bring herself to leave without a word of explanation, yes, at the last minute something in her had bridled and despite all the barriers and the silences, and her unalterable rigidity, and whatever guilt she must have felt, she'd tried to tell me this one thing, and she'd succeeded, she'd said the very thing she'd been meaning to tell me, obscurely and so to speak unawares, ever since she'd picked up the phone to invite me to this fateful party, and it had taken her all this time, it had taken her till now, to find the wherewithal and choose the moment to loosen the vise and slip me her hand and wave the handkerchief from the tower, and the words I caught were *roses* and *the only flowers I can bear to see cut*, and I had no idea what they meant. But I knew they contained a secret. I knew it with all my heart. They contained the thing she'd been trying to tell me and were just what I'd come to the party hoping to find. Five minutes later I was on the street and had kissed her goodbye, just like that, and had left her as if we'd said all there was to say, as if the so-called page had been turned, as if the page had been turned and I knew it.

·

I wandered home by unfamiliar streets. There was no point trying to find a taxi at that hour, in that suburb. In any case I was in the mood to walk. I wanted to be alone and take my time and move through space at my own tempo, not the forced pace of a car or mass transit, yes, I needed to feel the distance, the physical, mental, and personal space, that separated me just then from my own house, and for once I'd lost the craving for speed, with its bland reassurance that nothing happens while you pass from one point to another—as if the points themselves were all that mattered and were not in fact part of a single, identical, self-same, monotonous place, a place you can never leave. And in the cold I congratulated myself for what may have been the first time on having worn a turtleneck under my shirt, and all the while I was thinking, I never stopped thinking, of her little phrase, and I felt it crawling around inside me, inching up and down and burrowing through me, even as I relived the party and replayed all the evening's various events, which now struck me as essentially comic and harmless, nothing at any rate like the crushing disasters I'd been dreading. And what made me think I'd find all the powers and snares of the world ranged, as they say, against me at the party, all gathered in a conspiracy to expose my faults and my impotence? How thin-skinned I was, when you got right down to it: when you got right down to it, I was a clown! The whole thing was so intensely ridiculous, I deserved to be spanked. Or slapped. It hardly bore thinking about . . . and so roses were the only flowers that she could bear to see cut? What could she possibly mean? Certain conjectures sprang to mind, the words *rose* and *cut* naturally offered up no shortage of associations concerning women in general, and her in particular; but that didn't take me far. Really, that was no help at all. There was something else at work. Yes, something about my presence had effected a tiny shift in her being. Her little phrase had been addressed to me and me alone. And the same way I knew I hadn't dreamt it, I also knew beyond a shadow of a doubt that what she'd handed me was the key to her years of silence, a key that fit and opened just one lock, the lock of our story. And clearly this little phrase could never open anything else, and it occurred to me that if I kept coming up with explanations that circled back on themselves and glorified their own explanatory powers I'd be whistling in the dark, as they say, in this case and possibly in general—none of which brought me any closer to decoding the message that she had sent and, as it were, bestowed on me. In fact, I was as far off the mark as ever. As far as I was from home. And step by step I weighed her words and turned them over, I left no word unturned, and kept coming up empty-handed. And if I couldn't find some way out (I thought) this whole party would have been a farce, a bad farce, and I knew later I'd look back and tell myself it had all been in my head, that she hadn't, in the end, been trying to tell me *anything*—all because I was deaf to the mysterious invitation that she'd cast out to me like a lifesaver. And on my right there was a street sign pointing toward Paris, and I sighed with relief just to know that I wasn't lost, that I was in fact coming to a place I knew.

•

In an odd way, it seemed to me that I'd already lived through this scene—no, not that I had lived through it, but that the powerful scent of a forest after a rainstorm was flooding a sealed room in an apartment. This thought descended on me like a fog. It enveloped my mind all at once, and I actually found myself smiling at the odd swerve into absurdity that I'd taken from the subject at hand. No doubt physical and nervous exhaustion had something to do with it. At any rate, there it was. And as I walked I saw a bedroom in perfect detail, a bedroom assailed by the effluvia of wood and wet leaves, and in the bedroom the air was cool and vaguely fetid and the room was awash in the perfectly recognizable odor of acorns and moss and mushrooms even as I saw before me a table, chairs, a bed, a richly patterned rug, a painted ceiling, shelves lined with books. And (unless we had been lied to for centuries) these surroundings could hardly be called a forest, definitely not a forest after a rainstorm. You couldn't even call it a forest minus rain. Yes, it was simple and disorienting at the same time, and this vision filled me with happiness, with irrational joy, like a punchline: my eyes were completely at odds with my sense of smell, or vice versa, and I couldn't tell which sense was telling the truth and which was fooling the other (and the question seemed all the more pressing since in fact I have no sense of smell) and . . . *Mrs. Dalloway!*

•

The name surged up before my eyes, my blood caught fire, and the night began to dance around me, and it was all wrong, it made no sense, I couldn't think what the Virginia Woolf novel was doing here. What would I think of next? But it was as if an immense foreboding had taken hold of me and lifted me bodily from the earth and thrown me into the air. And my hair stood on end, as they say, and my legs actually started to wobble, and my blood sang out in my veins that I couldn't be entirely mistaken. A feeling like this couldn't lie, yes, her little phrase bore some connection to *Mrs. Dalloway*. In a heartbeat this revelation left me dazzled, and with each step I took it grew surer and more overwhelming, it came to me more and more clearly. And it was all because of that name. With one blow the name had opened a door I hadn't known was there and set free a towering stack of words, teetering toward me and telescoping outward. And it struck me that there'd been something in the book about red and white roses, something about a bouquet, though I couldn't think what, and it had to do with a reunion at a society dinner. Yes, at some large gathering a woman is reunited with a man she'd loved in her youth, and I couldn't think what his name was but she was the one who invited him, I was almost sure the invitation came from her, and they met again after years apart, and I couldn't think how the book ended, and that wasn't all, there was something else. Yes, now I remembered that she loved Virginia Woolf, and *Mrs. Dalloway* was one of her favorite books, possibly her very favorite at the time. One day she read me some passages out loud, but what I remembered was how moved she'd been when she closed the book, and that must have been when we first got together, and never, as far as I knew, had a book affected her so deeply, especially since this wasn't the kind of thing she read, yes, in those days she was always carrying around some thick history book, or some kind of multigenerational saga, and in any case I'd promised to read this book she loved, and in the end I didn't read it until years later, until after she left me, in fact. And when I read it it didn't seem all that great to me. It wasn't my kind of book either at that time in my life. I preferred Joyce's *Ulysses,* I thought of Virginia Woolf as working in his shadow. And now I felt gripped by a kind of madness, with every passing second I found new reasons for excitement, and just then everything around me glistened with new meaning and the pieces of the puzzle of my life seemed to fall magically into place, and I felt as though I were bursting, thousands of chips came clattering down in my head, and I actually heard them cascading down like coins in a slot machine, announcing that this was my lucky day: I'd hit the jackpot and life was a daring adventure. And there in the street I almost broke into a run for home. Yes, I had to make sure that I'd got it right, I had to make sure this wasn't just the last delusion of my fevered brain, and fifteen minutes later I was running up the stairs and dashed to my bookshelf without even taking off my coat to find the book by Virginia Woolf; but I couldn't find it, and I thought I was going to lose my mind—for a fraction of a second this was no laughing matter—and I had to rifle through all my shelves before I managed to find the little book with the gray cover that held all my hopes. And in a kind of delirium I tore through the story of Clarissa Dalloway and Peter Walsh, and I was not mistaken: "But she loved her roses . . . the only flowers she could bear to see cut."

•

The book couldn't have been more explicit. By the time I closed it I had my explanation. Yes, here in my hands were a thousand sentences that settled all the years' unanswered questions, settled them as if with a single word, and settled the answers to all the questions I'd never known to ask. And finally I knew why she'd called to invite me to that party and why I hadn't ever heard from her since she left. I thought I could even see to the bottom of her disappearance. Because from everything I read it was clear that *she* hadn't called to invite me to the party at all, the call had come from Mrs. Dalloway, or more accurately from the spirit of Mrs. Dalloway, which had possessed her in exactly the same way that the spirit of Ulysses had borne me up ever since she disappeared, from the very moment she disappeared, yes, it turned out I wasn't the only one who went in for this kind of maniacal sublimation, or even wholesale metamorphosis. Others had done the same, and she'd done it in spades, and it was unnerving, it was wonderful, and it all fit together too perfectly to be true—not that I was about to turn up my nose at any solution to the riddle that had tormented me from the moment of her disappearance up until that outlandish party, no matter if the so-called reality of the thing might be otherwise, no matter if my judgment and my memories might be false or even perverted by my impression of her. Who had the right to explain reality as I'd known it? I was human, too, in my way, and finally events, viewed in the light of Virginia Woolf's novel, were assuming a shape that I could tell myself made sense. They had happened for a reason, a reason I could understand, yes, for the first time they seemed, not absurd or chaotic or catastrophic, but logical and inspired. And, in a sense, redemptive, when I saw how she'd transposed these pages into real life. How, in spite of everything, having so little to work with, she'd taken Virginia Woolf's novel and, by a kind of miracle, tailored it to her own existence and followed the ethos that she glimpsed there, not just the broad strokes but the specifics of it too, and all the emotions and sensations that went with that ethos, feelings that she loved and (I was now convinced) darkly wished someday to make her own, as if something in the deepest and best part of her called out, *demanded*, to live an emotional life not rooted in fear, the fear to which the world seemed, and increasingly seems, bent on reducing us and whittling each of us down at every turn. The roses, the reunion, the party: it was all there, in black and white, and dozens of details that I recognized from her life leapt out at me, as they say, and each one seemed to be calling out to Clarissa Dalloway, as if each testified to a love that was magnificent and irreproachable and unique and spread her like a perfume through time and space, a perfume from which *she* had distilled her own essence, a perfume that I had no choice but to penetrate if I wanted to reach her, and I thought with a kind of terrified joy that if she had left me without a word of explanation it might be because she'd always hoped, without ever putting it into words, that we'd meet again, years later, to play the scene in which she would be Clarissa Dalloway reunited, for the duration of a party, with the man whom she had loved in her youth. And in the end hadn't everything conspired to bring that scene to life, to make it real—and so what *was* this thing called real life? After all, hadn't she done everything to make me cry out "'Clarissa! Clarissa!'" with the result that "she never came back . . . He never saw her again"? And did she think I wouldn't recognize her in this woman who "never lounged in any sense of the word," who was "straight as a dart, a little rigid in fact" and, at the same time "pure-hearted," terrified of death and capable of proclaiming that "what she liked was simply life"? It was her *all over*, and the more I thought about it the clearer it seemed that she'd found a real-life Richard Dalloway in the man who was the father of her daughter, someone "grey, dogged, dapper, clean," who could be described, again, from what I could see, as "pertinacious and dogged, having championed the downtrodden and followed his instincts." And remembering how they looked together, I imagined that she might very well repeat to herself inwardly, "it was a miracle that he should have married Clarissa." Nothing was missing, not even the daughter with "Chinese eyes in a pale face; an oriental mystery," whose photo she had shown me while we stood by the bay window. Not even the minutiae had been left to chance. All of it meant something. Taken as a whole, it expressed her desire to purge herself of roughness and mediocrity and rise to the condition of a novel, in any case that's how I saw it, how I wanted to see it, and when all was said and done I could even make out her image of me in the person of Peter Walsh, "with whom everything had to be shared, everything gone into" until it was "intolerable," Peter Walsh with "his old trick, opening a pocket-knife . . . always opening and shutting a knife when he got excited," who was "always in love, always in love with the wrong woman," who "put her into these states just by coming and standing in a corner . . . But why did he come then, merely to criticise?" Peter Walsh who was a "failure," uninterested in anything but "the state of the world," who "made terrible scenes" and had "no manners" and always lacked "the ghost of a notion what any one else was feeling." And there were plenty of other phrases that described and discomfited me and held up my own reflection with a wincing, altogether consuming clarity as gradually it dawned on me that the true mystery guest hadn't been me at all but this English novel, written in the 1920s, which had slipped its way into her life and changed its course and, therefore, the course of my own, and that in a larger sense literature was always getting invited into human history. And just when you think you've thought of everything, it occurred to me, you forget the book sitting right there on the bedside table.

•

So she'd left me without a word of explanation. It hardly mattered now. It was finally over and done with. Or was it? At any rate I never gave it another thought or felt at all bitterly toward her. I didn't feel any more rancor or despair. These feelings seemed to have been lifted like a spell—or rather transformed and refashioned into a kind of gratitude and tenderness, and actually I admired her and what she'd managed to do, yes, now that I saw and understood the high regard she felt for her own life, I started to see myself as collateral damage, as they say. Yes, looking past any question of cruelty, I discovered—I recognized with a shock— that all she wanted was "to save that part of life, the only precious part, this center, this ravishment that men let slip away, this prodigious joy that could be ours" (I'm quoting the publisher's blurb). The point was, in the face of a world that never stops pushing us around and trying to control us, she'd found a way to say no. She'd made her own way without choking off the lifeline that, if you ask me, is worth all the rest, worth more than all the rest put together, and in the end I was the one she brought in on her secret, and obviously she'd saved it for the end because the novel ends with the end of the party, just when Peter Walsh is getting up to leave, and what more could I ask? I had the explanation I'd come for, and it was worthy of our story, and it sold for twelve francs fifty at the time, and it was Sunday, October 14, 1990, and once again everything was happening on a Sunday: without any planning on my part, when I called the one who loved me despite my turtleneck-undershirts fifteen days had passed, almost to the hour, since that other phone call had given me my rude awakening, and I knew that from now on my existence was bound up with her and her delicate small hands, yes, I caught sight of the next chapter in my life, glimmering with possibilities and fresh prospects, because I'd finally turned over a new leaf, as they say. And naturally this new chapter would be full of falsehood and ambivalence, it would bear the same watermark as the rest, but it would lend a style of its own to our deeds and gestures, a style distinct enough to prove that something was actually taking place. And my heart beat with happy assurance, and on the other end of the line her voice already felt like a new embrace, a ripe hope, and as I went over all the less offensive vagaries of the party I looked out the window at the sky and the rooftops and the Sunday gray of the universe and it seemed to me that I, too, could acquire what Woolf called "the power of taking hold of experience, of turning it round, slowly, in the light," and I wanted it badly, and the next day when the radio announced that Delphine Seyrig had died, I knew in my heart that it had happened the day before, and not at Marienbad.

•

It sounds like nothing, but that was the day I bought a new lightbulb to replace the one in the bathroom. For I don't know how many weeks, maybe even months, the bulb had been burnt out and I'd never replaced it or made the slightest move in that direction. Despite the inconvenience—the absurdity—of trying to wash in the dark every morning and reaching around for the faucets without being able to see them and not being able to compose my face in the mirror, I had let things go on this way until it was second nature to me, although the one who loved me despite my turtleneck-undershirts complained whenever she stayed over, and I'd hear her muttering in the morning, cursing and accusing me of being hopelessly lazy and absentminded and (as time went on) self-absorbed. She'd say I never thought of her or worried how she might feel and, to put it bluntly, didn't love her since (as she said) we weren't in Peru, and replacing the bulb was the job of whoever found it burnt out, which was the least I could do for her, and at any rate I'd better not think *she* was going to take care of it. Because she wasn't. And the whole thing was just too stupid, she grumbled when I grabbed her around the waist. I said something about how it was no stupider than anything else in the world around us, and while she twisted out of my arms, half laughing, half furious at feeling herself hugged and manipulated this way, she snapped and said this was no reason to add to the general stupidity, and I nodded and promised her that the lightbulb would be changed that very day, and for months I hadn't lifted, as they say, a finger. And all at once the idea of buying a bulb, the actual urge to buy one, came to me, just like that, and in less time than it takes to write the words I'd screwed a magnificent 60-watt krypton over the bathroom sink, and I could just see

the satisfaction on her face when she'd discover
that I'd finally kept my word. And as I stood there,
jiggling the defective bulb in my hand to hear the
little noise of the filament, it hit me, for the first
time, that it was really and truly dead. And I wasn't
just thinking about some idiotic lightbulb. Far
from it. All of a sudden I understood that I was
able to replace this bulb because the light had
come back into some dark recess of my being so
that, in a way, having light in the bathroom made
sense. And what was the point of living if we
spent our lives fulfilling the desires of inanimate
objects? Was I supposed to change a bulb just because it was burnt out—to please a bathroom? I
had been right not to change it, I'd been right to
refuse to change it, insofar as changing it would
have meant nothing to me, yes, I'd had every reason to be stubborn, and it took that whole party
to make me see this, and it crossed my mind that
the whole party might never have taken place except to achieve this one shining, priceless—or at
any rate incontestible—result, my managing to
change a miserable lightbulb in a bathroom. And
standing there at the mirror I burst out laughing

at my reflection and at the face of a world so bent on problem-solving that it never bothers to find out what the problems mean to us, or ought to mean, and I thought of her electric kettle, which shocked her every third time she turned it on. How she'd cry out, startled, every time and promise to throw the kettle away as soon as we finished breakfast and every time did nothing. She always put this down to some obscure sentimental attachment, and now I understood that she wasn't holding on to the kettle itself, what she was really holding on to was the fact that it didn't work, and that changed everything, and I saw her from an angle I'd never imagined, her and possibly everything else that was going wrong just then on the planet, and I thought that to give her a new kettle, which I'd been thinking of doing, would be just the last thing to do, the least to the point and the least helpful to her when it came to taking hold of experience and turning it slowly in the light. Yes, a new kettle would just make things worse and distance her from herself, I thought, and when she came to my house in her irresistible navy blue dress with the white polka dots, which she knew fit my desire like a glove, I told her every odd thing that had gone racing through my mind while she was on her way over. And we went into the bathroom, which was now lit up like Versailles, and she looked at me tenderly, and with amusement, and I took her hands and she leaned in to kiss me and this kiss lasted for years, effacing all the turtleneck-undershirts on earth and all the confusion and desperation tucked away inside them.

•

At last I could breathe. Space and time came alive for me and seemed limitless, and in her arms the nights seemed bright with sun, and for the first time ever with a woman, it seemed to me, I could do no wrong and was doing everything right, and so four years later we had a little girl. It was now December 1994. And although I didn't know it at the time and don't know much about it now, that was precisely the year, the very month, that the space probe *Ulysses* reached the Sun after having traveled hundreds of millions of kilometers from the earth and from that day in October 1990 when things had finally started over for me and, you might say, come unstuck between us. Wasn't it wonderful? Wasn't it a marvel of astronomical proportions? According to the plan mapped out long ago on Earth, *Ulysses* was setting off on an immense tour of space before it circled back, sometime near 2001, toward the neighborhood of the Sun, and at the time I had no clue what was going on over my head, I hadn't the slightest suspicion, but during those years I, too, had the sensation of traveling away from the light and of plunging ineluctably into the empty darkness after she left me, soon after she had the child and, so to speak, accomplished her mission with me— and no, things didn't work out in the end. This time there were plenty of words of explanation, which kept me awake through more than one lonely afternoon, and something told me opportunity wouldn't call twice. It never does, I told myself, there will be no more mysterious invitations to endure and resist and *live* in the face of everything, and I was mistaken: after an evening spent drinking one beer after another by the light of a huge chandelier, the man who would become my publisher contracted with me to finish the text that I had just begun to write. It was supposed to tell, not the story of my life, which was worth about as much as anybody else's, but what my life had told me and what I thought I'd decoded of its language. And finally a book appeared in 2001, though the year was a matter of chance, and as incredible as it seems (and it does seem incredible to me) I had completed a slow and sweeping orbit through the space of my own life story hand in hand with a tiny space probe. And for the first time I seemed to approach, in words, a sun I could call my own. And Michel Leiris had been dead eleven years at the time, which meant that it had been more than fifteen years since he'd written that "literary activity, in its specific aspect as a mental discipline, cannot have any other justification than to *illuminate certain matters for oneself at the same time as one makes them communicable to others*, and that one of the highest goals . . . is to restore by means of words certain intense states, concretely experienced and become significant, to be thus put into words." Which was where, it seemed to me, everyone had to start.

IV

That might have been that. Ordinarily, it would have been. But one night I went to a party with the Lyonnaise, as I referred to a very young woman whose company had brightened certain hours of my life, and was told that somebody wanted to talk to me, was in fact eager to meet me and congratulate me on my book, and it was a woman, she was waiting for me at the bar—and it was Sophie Calle. At first I didn't quite put this information together; but as I crossed the room my excitement grew, I even felt a kind of thrill at the prospect of laying eyes on the woman in whose home, a dozen years before, my existence had been turned upside down, the woman whose intervention had set everything else in motion, yes, the story of the mystery guest came rushing back to me along with a feeling, perfectly preserved, which I realized had been drowned out by a thousand other memories, a feeling I'd forgotten over the years, and while I threaded my way toward the bar through the clusters of guests, I felt oddly as though I was reconnecting with the best part of my past and reliving what had already taken place, and I almost expected everything to start all over again. That's how uncanny it was, how full of portent, to be seeing her at another party, as if all the years and lives that had passed into and out of existence in the meantime had never been. As if, now that she'd straightened out the oysters in the kitchen, we were about to take up our conversation where we'd let it drop. At the same time I had no specific memory of what she looked like, and I wouldn't have recognized her on the street, and it wasn't until I was standing right in front of her that I was struck all over again by the openness of her smile, despite the heavy, serious black glasses that I didn't remember her wearing before, and the lock of hair was still falling over her forehead, and she was wearing a short dress, which showed off her breasts to great advantage, and I was so happy to see her, I was delighted, and I clasped her hand, and she said she was delighted to see me, too, and right away she started to talk in the most heartfelt terms about what I had written, and as she went on I began to realize that she had no idea who I was. My face didn't ring any bells, as they say, she obviously had no clue that I was one of her mystery guests, and things wavered and quivered around me, and slowly the room began to seem less and less real, and for a few seconds I had to clutch the stool beneath me with both hands, digging in with my nails, just to convince myself that everything wasn't going to blow away in a puff of smoke, including me, and the whole time I never stopped smiling, and I forced myself to concentrate on what she was saying, nodding my head the way I normally do, desperately trying to cover up a terrible suspicion that the whole length of my body was sliding softly down and puddling on the floor, right at my feet. And you're right (I said, trying to get a grip), what's important isn't that you say everything, but in the end that everything be said, and the only thrilling and really dangerous thing, I think, is to face what actually happened just as you witnessed it and, well, I don't want to sound pretentious—and to my relief this little riff kept playing itself out while the smile played on her lips, and her teeth were dazzling, and just then her whole face was spontaneous and present to me, and she gave off a kind of glow and, just as before, there seemed to be a spark passing between us. More than a spark—it was the bouquet, I told myself, it was always and forever and yet again the bouquet. Only this time it was a Big Bouquet, and in a flash it occurred to me that I might have wasted my days trying to puzzle out an expression that didn't make any actual sense, yes, suddenly the meaning of the expression struck me as inane and clumsy, it was gibberish, and point-blank, as they say, I asked whether she knew the origin of the expression "*c'est le bouquet*," and I begged her pardon, I didn't mean to interrupt, but there was something I had to tell her. The thing was, we'd already met once before. There was no reason she'd remember, but I had been one of her mystery guests, of all things. It must have been about ten years ago, strange and unlikely as that seemed, and then and there I sketched the events that led up to my playing the official unknown man at her birthday. And we could easily figure out which year it was because Michel Leiris had just died, and I remembered Hervé Guibert, so it was before he died, and she thought about it for a second and said it had to have been in 1990 because afterward she'd left France. And the whole time I spoke and went into all the details and generally laid my cards, as they say, on the table, her eyes never left my face and her gaze plunged into mine with all the force of her attention, and I was able to tell her everything, and I confessed what a humiliation the whole thing had been at the time, especially the moment when I found out that she took a picture of the presents everybody brought her without ever opening them. And at the word *humiliation* I saw her eyes cloud over. She looked troubled. She had no memory of me at all. She said she was sorry, sorry and surprised, and I got the distinct impression that she thought I was making it all up. And I told her it made perfect sense that she'd forgotten me since I'd been a rotten mystery guest. In fact, I'd left her party almost as soon as I got there. She was the one who had played a huge and unexpected role in my life, and when you got right down to it I was, as they say, beholden to her. And in a certain sense (I told her) it would even be fair to say I'm one of your works, and from the look she gave me I could tell this kind of flattery left her cold, and this look of hers bowled me over, it made me so happy. With every passing moment she seemed more wonderful to me, more than wonderful, she seemed worthy of—something, I didn't know what, and to change the subject I asked whether, in the end, I'd brought her luck for the year, and she told me that she'd left to move to the United States and had married a man named Greg.

•

This had nothing to do with me, obviously, but the coincidence was striking, and just then I couldn't help thinking she might identify my name with the name of her husband and, laughing, I told her that she'd better not amputate my *goire*. As if I knew we'd be seeing more of each other. And (apropos of her husband) she asked whether I'd seen the film of their picaresque wedding in Las Vegas. I admitted that I'd only heard about it, yes, after this business with the mystery guest and the Margaux, I'd kept my distance from her work, and all these years I'd tried to know as little as possible about her reputation, I even skimmed over her name when I saw it in the press, and took the firm position that nothing she might photograph or exhibit or write could ever teach me anything about her that I didn't already know, all too well—and anyway, contemporary art, as they say, didn't speak to me. Or rather, I didn't care for what it had to say. In this it was like most other forms of cultural endeavor. No doubt that spoke to my own ignorance, I qualified as I refilled our glasses with red wine, and if I was trying to provoke her I was barking up the wrong tree, as they say, because she didn't seem the least bit offended by what I was saying. On the contrary, my attitude seemed to please her. She seemed to like it, in fact. All I knew was what a friend had told me: that in one scene of her movie she and her husband filmed each other playing truth or dare, or something like truth or dare, and at some point she made a gesture, I can't remember now what it was supposed to be, but she lowered the camera and stopped filming, I think, and it was as if suddenly she'd laid down her arms and proposed a truce—a truce with none of the conditions that everyone always imposes on everyone else, whether they're in a couple or not. And it was unwatchable, according to this friend (who was having problems of his own with his wife), because her husband refused to give it up. He kept filming and held on to the camera and hid behind it, as if he couldn't or wouldn't see, as if he refused to see, that she'd tried to get out of her turn, that she'd ventured out into the open and waved the white handkerchief. And this friend had told me that he understood what was going on in the husband's head, he even sympathized, but at that moment he desperately wanted the husband to do something, anything, just so long as he didn't leave her there that way, just so long as he didn't leave *himself* there that way, and in the end things went very badly with his wife, and he told me that this was the shortest, most tragic, and in the end the most radical, love scene he'd ever come across on film. For the first time someone had captured the impossible demand that women make on men, and men's impossible acquiescence, and this curse that separates them, which is familiar to us all and weighs down on us like a kind of despair and—I was sorry, I was talking too much and I hadn't even seen the film. I'd never been into movies. And she was about to light a cigarette, and she said that she'd really like to meet this friend of mine. And all at once I saw her eyes on the verge of tears, I mean tears on the verge of her eyes, I can't think how you say it, and this emotion took me completely by surprise. And it's not as if she was trying to hide it, or impose it on me, it was just there, like a kind of vast sorrow, naked and simple, and I sat there and waited for it to pass. I knew there was nothing to say at that moment, I didn't even try to think of anything to say, and she took a few drags on her cigarette and had a sip of her wine and then she looked right at me and gave me a dazzling smile that seemed just then like an artwork of its own, torn out of her, and she asked me in a bright, cheerful voice whether I was working on anything new, and I told her that an astrologer had predicted a few years earlier that one day I'd write a book and it would enjoy some success and then I'd never write another word.

·

She herself was doing a project with an astrologer. She was also putting together a big show, and she was full of stories, each crazier and more ludicrous, heartbreaking, and extravagant than the last. (*Extravagant* was her word.) And it seemed like centuries since I'd spoken with a woman so simply and freely, as if we spoke the same language. And it was unfettered—that's what it was:

absolutely unfettered—and this language con-
sisted of everything we'd been through and overcome and turned into stories, little stories with
facets we could polish up to make ourselves feel
alive. And now and then my gaze lingered on her
shoulders and on her breasts and lips, and she noticed and didn't stop smiling, and there was something talmudic in her smile, and I fought the urge
to tuck back that distracting lock of hair, which
reminded me uncomfortably of my turtlenecks, so
that I could see her forehead and bask in the light
of her whole face, and she told me that she was
obviously going to invite me to her next birthday:
she'd be turning fifty. She said this serenely, without the least twinge of self-consciousness, but I
felt a sudden pang. It was as if a passing shadow
had slipped into the sunshine between us. Fifty,
she had said fifty. But that was impossible. I hadn't
given her age a second's thought. I hadn't paid it
any attention. That's what was bothering me—
and it was absurd, she couldn't be fifty. It didn't
make any sense. I was forty-three, and she seemed
so light and graceful, even in an odd way childlike.
And it wasn't her age that upset me, I realized. It

wasn't her age today, at that party. No, it was what her age suddenly told me about the future, something horrific and unbearable, something scandalous. That was the thing: in five years she'd be fifty-five, then sixty, and this vision struck me as hopeless and impossible to face, as if for the first time I were glimpsing my own old age, as if I were racing toward it, and while I replied happily that I'd love to come to her birthday I felt myself wanting to close my eyes to the cruelty of existence, and I felt another little phrase taking form, in the blink of an eye, against the phrase that had opened such prospects for me years before, that had handed me the hope and innocence of the future on a silver platter, and just then time seemed to me the worst mystery guest of all. And saying goodbye to her a little while later, so that I could leave with the woman who'd brought me to the party, I kissed her softly on the lips as if this simple kiss had the power to undo the injustice and disgrace of what lies crouched in wait for us all.

•

She called me three days later. Something extravagant had happened, she said, something insane and unheard of. She still couldn't believe it (I could hear her laughing to herself on her end of the line), and she hoped she hadn't caught me at a bad moment, but it just had to be a sign. My story about the mystery guest had intrigued her and she'd gone to the book where she kept a record of all the birthday presents she'd received over the years, and she checked to see whether she could find the Margaux, and she hadn't found a trace of it, not in the chapter on the year 1990 or anywhere else, and I was about to defend myself, I was going to say this was impossible, that this trial would never end, but in a rush she told me that, just to put her mind at ease, she'd gone down into the basement where she stored her work, and I wasn't going to believe this, it was extravagant, but she'd rummaged around all over. She'd spent hours turning the place upside down although she had plenty of other things to do and I knew it wasn't as if she was looking for ways to kill time. In any event, it seemed clear to her that I couldn't have been lying and she wanted to have a clear conscience, at least, and in fact (I already knew what she was about to say) way up high on a shelf she'd found a bottle of wine still wrapped in tissue paper, and it was a 1964 Margaux, and it had to be mine, and she'd found it! Solemnly she read me the label over the phone: "*Grand Cru Classé—Château du Tertre—Appellation Margaux Controlée—Mise en Bouteille au Château—Proprietaire.*" And hearing her what could I say except that it really was extravagant? And, at the same time, it had all happened so long ago that I didn't quite know how I felt about it, or whether this bottle still had any meaning for me. But now it meant something to her and she couldn't get over the idea that the bottle had sat there all those years in the dark on a shelf, she was so organized and painstaking. She told me never to mention it again, I had to promise, and I promised, but this was the first time she'd ever been in the wrong about her own work, and yet she had an excuse—there was no name on the bottle saying who had brought it, and since she didn't know me she'd thought the mystery guest had brought her one of the two gift certificates that had turned up the morning after the party (which no one had ever cashed in). Naturally she assumed that one of them had to have come from me, and that was what she'd written in her book, and as soon as she hung up the phone she was going to send me a corrected copy, and the whole thing had obviously been an adventure for her, and I could hear her voice crack with excitement at the end of the line, and she kept saying how extravagant it was, and I heard her pacing, never standing still, because her heels were echoing and clacking on what must have been tile, and in fact she was in the kitchen, and she was desperately trying to figure out where she could put the bottle that was dark but where she could still see it, and I just had to come and look, right away. She couldn't bear the responsibility on her own for another minute. And I laughed and told her I was on my way, and in the taxi that took me there, to the house where everything had started eleven years before, the driver didn't tell me any stories, in fact he was on the brusque side, and on the radio a so-called journalist informed us that the U.S. military had just hired the writer-director of *Die Hard* to help work out strategic scenarios, so that, if I understood correctly, fiction was being called to the official aid and reinforcement and rescue of real life, as if real

life weren't always fiction in the first place. And
while I looked out the window at the street I'd already walked down, I thought how many events
were taking place everywhere, I thought of the beings and things and my own wayward and basically
lucky life, and we pulled up, and while I paid the
fare in a different currency from the one I'd paid
in the first time I found myself wondering what
book was sitting on her bedside table. All of a sudden nothing mattered to me more.

•

One year later I was at Erquy, on the road to Plurien,
Côtes d'Armor, and it was warm for early February
and I was hunting for seashells on the empty beach,
thinking about this story of the mystery guest that
I'd decided to tell, because I'd made up my mind I
was going to give the lie to the astrologer and all the
stars—and here's the thing: at the very moment
when I wrote "It was the day Michel Leiris died,"
unbeknownst to me, the directors of NASA and the
European Space Agency agreed to extend the mission of the space probe *Ulysses* until 2008. Yes, so
that in the very month of February 2004, after four-
teen years of good and loyal service and two suc-

cessful rendezvous with the Sun, they were granting it a special third pass, just when I sat down to write again and extend my own voyage of discovery. And when I heard the news I burst out laughing, I saw stars, and it felt as though I was the one who'd been granted a special dispensation, and I no longer knew what to think, it was all beyond me. What are the odds that my destiny should be bound up, or at any rate synchronized, with a little fifty-seven-kilogram space probe? I got dizzy just thinking about it, and a little bit scared, and I called Sophie to share this last coincidence with her and tell her that it seemed far-fetched—*tiré par les cheveux*, as they say—even to me. Who would believe me? And in a calm voice she pointed out that, from the age of eight, I'd been pulling reality's hair and adding its scalps to my belt and I had no reason to complain, and she was looking forward to seeing me, and, hanging up, I asked her whether she happened to weigh exactly fifty-seven kilos.

•

This was in fact the case.